FC2950.A1 M2 2003
0/34/0916/1932
Maclure,

Quebec i(
challen(
c20(

QUEBEC IDENTITY

Quebec Identity

The Challenge of Pluralism

JOCELYN MACLURE

TRANSLATED BY PETER FELDSTEIN

McGill-Queen's University Press
Montreal & Kingston · London · Ithaca

To my parents, Céline and Luc

© McGill-Queen's University Press 2003
ISBN 0-7735-2553-X (cloth)
ISBN 0-7735-2598-X (paper)
Legal deposit second quarter 2003
Bibliothèque nationale du Québec
Printed in Canada on acid-free paper.

This book has been published with the help of a grant from the Canadian Federation for the Humanities and Social Sciences, through the Aid to Scholarly Publications Program, using funds provided by the Social Sciences and Humanities Research Council of Canada.

Translation of this book was made possible by a grant from the Translation Program of the Canada Council for the Arts.

McGill-Queen's University Press acknowledges the support of the Canada Council for the Arts for our publishing program. We also acknowledge the financial support of the Government of Canada through the Book Publishing Industry Development Program (BPIDP) for our publishing activities.

National Library of Canada Cataloguing in Publication

Maclure, Jocelyn, 1973 –
   Quebec identity: the challenge of pluralism/Jocelyn Maclure; translated by Peter Feldstein.

   Translation of: Récits identitaires.
   Includes bibliographical references and index.
   ISBN 0-7735-2553-X (bound)
   ISBN 0-7735-2598-X (pbk)

   1. Pluralism (Social sciences) – Quebec (Province) 2. Canadians, French-speaking – Quebec (Province) – Ethnic identity.
   3. Nationalism – Quebec (Province) 4. Multiculturalism – Quebec (Province) I. Title.

FC2950.A1M3213 2003   306.44'6'09714   C2003-900338-8

Typeset in Palatino 10/13
by Caractéra inc., Quebec City

Contents

Foreword CHARLES TAYLOR vii

Preface to the English Edition xi

Translator's Preface xvii

Acknowledgments xix

Introduction 3

1 Cultural Fatigue and Arrested Development: The Melancholy Nationalists 19

2 Towards a New Representation of Ourselves: Guy Laforest and Jocelyn Létourneau 61

3 Identity within the Limits of Reason Alone: Anti-nationalism and Political Universalism 86

4 From Identity to Democracy: Quebec and the Challenge of Pluralism 119

APPENDICES

1 Quebec Figures 147

2 Quebec Institutions, Events, and Concepts 159

Notes 169

Index 209

Foreword

This essay constitutes an important contribution to the ongoing debate about identity in Quebec. *Quebec Identity* crystallizes what has, until now, been an inchoate change of course taking place in our society. Many Quebecers of all ages, but especially members of the younger generations, have come to feel increasingly uncomfortable with the polarized, dogmatic confrontation between sovereigntists and federalists. Despite the continuous tallying of economic advantages and disadvantages on either side of the question, everyone has always implicitly understood that the debate is not fundamentally about economics but, rather, identity.

While one side would claim that Quebecers can only resolve their paralyzing ambiguity and regain their true identity by founding a new and independent country, the other would riposte by laying narrow-mindedness and exclusion squarely at the door of nationalism itself, denying its value as a basis for identity. But what both positions seemed to share is the premise that identity must be something clear, unified, stable, set in stone. Yet it has become evident that many people, especially youth – and particularly those who have travelled – no longer relate to this paradigm. They are

Foreword

only too well aware of how their own identities serve as loci of ceaseless debate, evolution, and conflict; in a word, how plural their identities tend to be. They do not feel comfortable with a univocal, fixed *québécité* ("Quebec-ness") or with an outright rejection of the nation as a source of identity. The time was approaching when their perspective would take its rightful place in our debate, and by now it has.

All that was missing was a sustained theoretical formulation of this new way of seeing. With *Quebec Identity*, Jocelyn Maclure has given us a most clear and convincing one. But he has done more than that. In this field of scholarship, the tone of the writer is as important as the content. A certain tone has characterized debates over identity issues, a contemptuous, polemical tone, in which the antagonists try to discredit each other's definitions by portraying them as petty and intolerable. Some sovereigntists, for example, present a dual allegiance to Quebec and Canada as evidence of immaturity or even cowardliness; as for the Trudeau federalists, their rhetoric has often led them to demonize nationalism as such. But definitions of identity develop out of a hermeneutics of our deep experience, and for that reason they deserve a degree of respect, even when we think they are mistaken. The arrogance of the polemical tone is bad enough; even worse is how it causes people to reject one another's ideas out of hand, making any exchange of interpretations impossible.

What is remarkable about Jocelyn Maclure's work is the respectful, comprehending tone he adopts when discussing positions of which he is critical. Because of this characteristic, his book does more than lay out a theoretical framework for renewed discussion of identity issues; it sets the tone for that discussion by its own example. Whether or not one agrees with his detailed accounts of "melancholy nationalism" and

Foreword

"cosmopolitan internationalism," one immediately recognizes in them a new way of apprehending the unavoidable existential debate in Quebec around questions of nation and nationalism. The successful accomplishment of this necessary enterprise demands all the sensitivity and subtlety of this young author: his ability to discern the human experience underlying the most polemical of statements; his generosity towards his many partners in the discussion; and his keen sense of the multiple and diverse voices involved in interpreting the complex, shifting reality of contemporary Quebec. This is a study of great hermeneutic and theoretical value, one that breaks new and potentially fertile ground for research and discussion. It is a significant contribution to the reconstitution of Quebec.

Charles Taylor

Preface to the English Edition

According to the columnist Graham Fraser, English Canada's understanding of who Quebecers are always seems to be behind by a decade.[1] I do not know whether Fraser's claim is fully accurate, but his examples are persuasive: even after the Quiet Revolution in the 1960s, Quebec society continued to be seen elsewhere in Canada as a province oppressed under the weight of its Catholic priesthood; a decade later, the fully democratic Parti Québécois (PQ) was conflated with the militant separatist and at times terrorist Front de Libération du Québec (FLQ). One thing I do know is that the question of identity has been the subject of heated debate in the last twenty years in Quebec, and especially so since the 1995 referendum. Francophones, aboriginal peoples, anglophones, Quebecers from abroad, and Quebecers born in Quebec of immigrant parents are asking questions such as: Who is an "authentic" Quebecer? Is Quebec a nation, and if so, what kind of nation is it? How can the French language be promoted without encroaching on individual rights? What is the status of the historical national minorities, namely, the anglophone community and the eleven First Nations, who share Quebec's territory with the francophone majority?

What kind of rights and resources must be provided to immigrants in order to facilitate their integration (instead of their assimilation or ghettoization)? As we can see, the challenge of pluralism appears to be the theme underlying these intertwined issues.

Unfortunately, one particular voice, on one particular occasion, has echoed louder than all the others in the rest of Canada – Jacques Parizeau's, when he notoriously blamed "money and the ethnic vote" for the Yes side's defeat in the 1995 referendum. While the government and numerous academics, writers, artists, and citizens had been claiming that there are many different ways to be an authentic Quebecer and that Quebec's identity is civic rather than ethnic, Parizeau revived the old and obsolete dichotomy between the *pure laine* (old-stock French Canadians) and the anglophone and allophone "others." He resigned the next day, as his statement was immediately repudiated by most leaders of public opinion in Quebec.

The more general trend of inclusion and openness at play in the province since the 1980s[2] was reflected in new premier Lucien Bouchard's vision of Quebec. Bouchard was not interested in distinguishing among Quebecers by cultural background; he was a nationalist and a sovereigntist who thought that authenticity did not hinge on ethnic origin (being from a French-Canadian background) or political orientation (being in favour of Quebec independence).

Yet ironically, the issue of authenticity contributed to Bouchard's political demise in January 2001, when he resigned in reaction to the comments of Yves Michaud, a well-known PQ supporter. Whistling Parizeau's favourite tune, Michaud essentially said that the absence of support for sovereignty in electoral ridings almost exclusively inhabited by allophones was proof of intolerance towards the francophone majority. He thereby ignored other perfectly valid conclusions that might be drawn from the referendum results. For example, he never thought of blaming the majority of women or senior citizens among the francophones themselves who had voted against secession. This type of nationalist, a minority within both Quebec society and the PQ, tends to reify the "them" and to homogenize the "us." But as I will argue in chapter 4 of this book, in late modernity the boundaries of "us" and "them" are porous, shifting with the changing problems that people face in their lives.

Michaud's comments generated heated public debate in Quebec, and the National Assembly unanimously condemned them.[3] But the unfortunate effect of restaging the debate on allophone authenticity was to obscure (especially outside Quebec) the continuous symbolic and institutional transformation of identity that has taken place since the 1980s. In the social imaginary, the traditional markers of identity have been problematized and pluralized by Quebecers born in Quebec and abroad, and the categories of hybridity, transculturalism, and *métissage* have emerged as dominant languages of (self-) representation.[4] At the institutional level, the Quebec model of liberalism and democratic pluralism revolves around three principles. In the government's vision, Quebec is

- a society in which French is the common language of public life;
- a democratic society where everyone is expected and encouraged to participate and contribute;
- a pluralist society that is open to multiple influences, within the limits imposed by the need to respect fundamental values and the need for inter-group exchanges.[5]

Preface to the English Edition

These principles are enacted through a policy of "interculturalism," which strives to recognize and value cultural diversity as well as to promote cross-cultural deliberation and mediation.[6] Moreover, the government of Quebec's handling of the negotiations with the Cree over the revision of the James Bay Agreement ("The Peace of the Braves") and the current negotiations with the Innu point towards the establishment of more post-imperial relationships between Quebec and the First Nations that have very few precedents. These negotiations take the ancestral rights of the aboriginal nations as a given and do not attempt to extinguish them. The point here is obviously not to claim that Quebec's way of managing diversity is problem-free, but to acknowledge the structural and symbolic transformations of identity here in the past twenty years. Any serious appraisal of Quebec identity and citizenship policies must now take these transformations into consideration.

The dialogue between Quebec and the rest of Canada is probably more strained now than at any time since the 1976–84 period (which coincided with the rise and fall of René Lévesque's PQ government, the first referendum, the patriation of the Constitution, and the end of the Trudeau era). Quebec's political weight in the Canadian federation has declined since the 1995 referendum (won by a slim majority of No votes), and the Liberal government in Ottawa now has all the leeway necessary to dictate the terms of the Quebec-Canada relationship. It is a truism to say that much of the Canadian constitutional "impasse" turns upon a great deal of mutual misunderstanding. As with any disagreement or conflict, the crucial first step in resolving it is to put oneself in the other's shoes, to see things from the other's perspective while trying to gain distance from one's own identity/

Preface to the English Edition

ies, values, commitments, and interests. As a critical examination of the main identity narratives that have shaped Quebec's self-image since the 1950s and as an exploration of how this identity can be imagined differently, this book can perhaps help to clarify some aspects of Quebec's past and contemporary identity. In so doing, it may remove some unnecessary impediments to the restoration of a constructive dialogue between Quebec and the rest of Canada. I look forward to similar books about Canadian identity and politics being translated into French and published in Quebec.

JM
Quebec City
20 October 2002

Translator's Preface

It is surely fitting, and was perhaps to be expected, that the most difficult translation problem in a book on identity in Quebec would be the word "Québécois." The dilemma posed by this word is that different people apply it to the identity of "Quebecness" in different ways. In its most inclusive and geographical sense, the term refers simply to the people of Quebec, and for this sense we have the word "Quebecer" (or adjectivally, "Quebec"), just as the people of New York are called "New Yorkers." In keeping with the author's own inclusive intent, I have used this term where the context allowed. But I would be blurring an obvious distinction made by many people, in and outside of academe, if I ignored another referent of "Québécois": the French-speaking or francophone Quebecers, formerly called the "French Canadians" (the latter term having largely fallen into disuse since the Quiet Revolution). Within the second meaning are often (but not always) included Quebecers from other backgrounds who feel a strong identification with this place; they have adopted French as their habitual language, or have put down roots here, or align themselves with a political agenda for Quebec's future, or simply feel "Québécois," whatever it represents for them. Shades and nuances aside, though, this second meaning is quite different from the first; it is the meaning clearly intended by most of

Translator's Preface

the "melancholy nationalists" studied in chapter 1, and I would err if I glossed it over with a blanket use of "Quebecer." I have kept the French term "Québécois" for this usage and had the author vet each instance of it. As these comments suggest, and as this book will make much clearer, the translator (or any Quebecer, or anyone anywhere for that matter) steps onto slippery terrain whenever identities are the topic of discussion. I can only ask the indulgence of those who feel that this terminological choice stands to be improved.

I have translated the terms "francophone," "anglophone," and "allophone" by their cognates, as is common in Quebec, to mean people whose first or most comfortable language of expression is French, English, or anything else, respectively.

For quotations originally in French, published English translations are provided where available. However, many of the quoted sources have never appeared in English before, and the translations of these are my own.

I would like to thank Michelle Braiden for typing the manuscript, and Siobhan Ua'Siaghail for assisting with translation and research on the glossary. My colleague Raymond Robitaille amiably agreed to puzzle over many translation issues with me, while Susanne Harwood and Ted Blodgett, fellow members of the Literary Translators' Association of Canada, pointed me in the right direction on one phrase, "difficulté d'être." Elizabeth Hulse edited the manuscript with great skill, and Joan McGilvray and Aurèle Parisien of McGill-Queen's provided helpful editorial support. Most of all, it was the author Jocelyn Maclure's keen sensitivity to the issues of translation which made the whole process a smooth and pleasant one. My thanks to him for responding with unending alacrity and incisiveness to my continual questions. No translator could hope for better than the kind of "reciprocal elucidation" that has led us to this English version of *Récits identitaires*.

Peter Feldstein

Acknowledgments

At first sight, the writing of a book of this kind might seem to represent the quintessence of solitude and introspection, a monologue with the self. Nothing could be further from the truth; from start to finish, it has been a dialogical activity. That being the case, I have many people to acknowledge here. First and foremost among them are my parents, Luc Maclure and Céline Miron, whose warm-hearted support never wavered. It is with great pleasure that I dedicate this book to them. Isabelle Dumont, in addition to her comments and suggestions, offered me all the encouragement and support necessary to carry off such a project. Her generosity was for me a constant source of inspiration. If a little of that generosity shines through in these pages, this undertaking will not have been in vain.

The contributions of Guy Laforest and James Tully were invaluable. Starting with my undergraduate work at Université Laval, Professor Laforest has offered me all the support and guidance necessary for academic success. Furthermore, his rigorous comments greatly improved the manuscript. I cannot overemphasize the importance, both intellectual and personal, of my meeting James Tully, who became my academic supervisor at the University of Victoria. It was one of

Acknowledgments

those special and rare encounters that cause a person to diverge from his established itinerary and widen his field of possible options. This essay also greatly benefited from serious and attentive readings by Jocelyn Létourneau and Alain-G. Gagnon, for which I thank them.

The enthusiasm and comments of Marie-Josée Deblois were of great utility, as were the discussions I had with my friends Eddy Vo-Quang, Dimitri Karmis, Nigel De Souza, and David Owen. I would like to thank Stéphan Gervais and Alain-G. Gagnon of the McGill University Quebec Studies Program, to whom I am grateful for encouraging me to make Quebec a focus of my thinking and for giving me every opportunity to do so. I would also like to thank Charles Taylor. There can be no greater honour for a young student of political philosophy in Quebec than to have his first book prefaced by Professor Taylor. It was a great pleasure to collaborate with McGill-Queen's University Press, and I particularly want to acknowledge Aurèle Parisien's kind support and very effective work. The art of translation is difficult and challenging, and I feel lucky that my manuscript fell into the hands of Peter Feldstein, a very creative and circumspect translator. My thanks also go to Pierre Skilling for the appendices. Finally, my regards to Dave, Sandy, Damélie, Edward (my godson, whose birth preceded the French edition of this book by a few months), Sébastien, and Henri (and their respective families) and everyone else whose contribution unfortunately cannot be mentioned here individually. I know you are well aware of how great your value and importance is to me; there is a little of each one of you in this book.

Jocelyn Maclure

QUEBEC IDENTITY

Introduction

> We cannot define the nature of a nation if we ignore the incessant work of the people who interpret its existence.
>
> Fernand Dumont

Identity as a topic gets a lot of copy; a great many writers and theorists, in Quebec and elsewhere, have made it their muse. University disciplines and theoretical approaches intertwine and overlap as they endeavour to map out the terrain, to chart a course for us through the labyrinth of contemporary identity. Thus philosophy, political science, sociology, psychology, history, anthropology, geography, literary studies, and cultural studies, as well as hermeneutic, phenomenological, neo-Kantian, Marxist, feminist, post-colonialist, and post-structuralist approaches, all cross-fertilize and refute one another in a grand enterprise of conceptual exploration. Later in this introduction, I will attempt to discern the sources of this burgeoning interest in identity issues. Quebec is exemplary of the phenomenon; its society, composed of a national francophone majority, a national anglophone minority, eleven aboriginal nations, and a multiplicity of Quebecers from other backgrounds, is at once multinational, multicultural, and hybrid.[1] So-called identity politics and politics of recognition, which have become central to the process whereby identities are conceptualized, have long been fundamental to the dynamics of Quebec society.

For an observer to attempt to encapsulate the essence of his or her own historical epoch is always perilous, but surely it is not too bold to assert that Quebec is currently in the throes of an exceptionally intense interrogation of its own identity – a process of self-interpretation and renarration. Although no one can say for certain how the society will be reconfigured by it, we can be sure that new tropes of identity will come to augment – and thus to challenge and confront – the dominant representations of *québécité*, of "Quebec-ness." This fascination in Quebec with identity issues is not an arcane debate among university academics; it is a live concern that cuts across class, sex, and generational barriers, affecting every citizen who has to live with identity indeterminacy on a daily basis.[2] And so we have seen a proliferation of articles, books, and conferences on the distinct but intimately related issues of identity, nationality, culture, language, citizenship, gender, and so on. For many observers, the intensity of this self-examination in Quebec evidences a chronic insecurity complex; it is a product of Quebecers' atavistic inability to firmly take charge of their own affairs. Such observers would say that perpetual identity anxiety is the price that one must pay to enjoy the comforts of ambivalence.

In my view, however, the ongoing ferment in Quebec around identity issues is better explained by factors both exogenous and endogenous to Quebec society. First, it gains impetus from a world dynamic characterized by the globalization of markets and means of communication, by an unparalleled compression of time and space. What becomes of minority nations such as Quebec when Keynesian regulation of erstwhile "domestic economies" is increasingly a thing of the past, and when the mass media steamrolls over the cultural boundaries between nations? How can we

Introduction

delimit the authenticity of a nation when international migratory movements are making polyethnicity and hybridity the rule rather than the exception, and when "nationals," of whatever country, are finding themselves identifying with and belonging to an increasing number of regional, international, and virtual communities? In a similar vein, how are the plural identity horizons and histories of contemporary writers forcing us to redefine the concept of "national" literature? Writers in Quebec, not unlike other citizens but perhaps more intensely, are continually forging and reforging the cultural specificity of their home territory, rather than communing at the altar of either national authenticity or rootless cosmopolitanism; and they do so by drawing on their eclectic sources of memory, belonging, and identity (local, national, transnational). All these phenomena, which I shall analyze at greater length in chapter 4, make the ego and the alter, the self and the other, more difficult to distinguish – thoroughly indissociable, in fact.

Second, and endogenously, this process of self-interpretation has much to do with Quebec's problematic status within the Canadian federation. Nothing at present, at least in the short and medium term, presages the arrival of a genuine ethic of dialogue between Quebec and Ottawa. Some twenty years have gone by since the promises of constitutional renewal brandished by Pierre Elliott Trudeau at the height of the referendum campaign, when the No forces were faltering, and their easy victory looked as though it might turn into an upset defeat. As we know, these guarantees of constitutional change led to the unilateral patriation of the Constitution, a curtailment of the powers of the Quebec parliament (Assemblée Nationale), and the institution of a pan-Canadian Charter of Rights and Freedoms. Both Quebec and Anglo-Canadian observers agree that the events of 1981–82 represent a Canadianization of the federation; that is to say, a deliberate attempt to substitute Canada for Quebec as the primary object of allegiance in Quebecers' hearts.[3] Yet a large majority of Quebecers have never denied their Canadianness, even if for many it was upstaged by a primary identification with Quebec. Only a minority of sovereigntists believe that Quebecers' allegiance to Canada is merely accessory or transitory. In fact, their "Canadian dream," in Guy Laforest's phrase, was precisely to live in a binational Canada, one in which their way of identifying with Quebec would not be perceived as a vice or a heresy.[4] Though not obliterated, the hope of one day realizing that dream was rudely shaken by the events of 1981–82. It has become increasingly difficult for Quebec to budge the symbolic edifice built up by Trudeau and his political lineage. Since 1982, Quebec has been up against a quasi-systematic policy of non-recognition.[5]

A reminder of the solidity of this edifice was provided by the Meech Lake episode. Meech, it may be recalled, was perceived as a corrective for the 1982 adoption of the Constitution Act without Quebec's consent. Its failure added insult to the injury of 1982 and served as a powerful demonstration of the degree to which an individualist, uninational vision of the country had become ingrained in the Anglo-Canadian symbolic universe. This shift is what led the philosopher Charles Taylor to state before the Bélanger-Campeau Commission, "We can envisage Quebec, at least as a starting point for this reflection, as a society free of all previous commitments, which is preparing to give itself structures that suit it and which, as a consequence, is thinking of proposing to one or some possible partners new arrangements that would be of common interest ... On 23 June 1990, the 1867 Constitution died morally in Quebec. It is necessary to create anew."[6]

Introduction

The situation has hardly improved since 1990. On the contrary, the 1995 no-win referendum further polarized the existing positions, which seem united now only by the intensity of their acrimony. Tragically, Taylor's unequivocal verdict has lost none of its currency. The two camps, both greatly lacking in political imagination, have yet to put forward positions that can advance the debate, however marginally, towards breaking the constitutional deadlock. On one side, the separatists are too taken up with their quest for normality to understand that a large majority of Quebecers would like their government to help the federal government and the other provinces comprehend the multinational character of Canada. They seem closed to the idea that the Supreme Court's decision in the reference on Quebec secession has altered the playing field for constitutional change in Canada.[7] Yet this decision suggests a radically different way of looking at Canadian constitutionalism and relations between Quebec, the rest of Canada, and the Native peoples.[8] It will be recalled that the Supreme Court of Canada ruled in 1998 that the Canadian constitutional order is built on a permanent tension between the principles of democracy, the rule of law and constitutionalism, federalism, and respect for minorities, and that any demand from Quebec, having obtained the assent of a clear majority of Quebecers, while guaranteeing that the interests of dissident minorities were taken into consideration, cannot be ignored by the government of Canada and the other Canadian provinces. On the contrary, Quebec's observance of such a procedure would impose on the other members of the federation a "correlative duty" to negotiate over the proposals put forward by Quebec.

Meanwhile the federalists – who actually wear the name rather badly – provide daily illustrations of their inability to recognize Quebec and the aboriginal peoples in the terms used by the latter to define their identity, and to provide them with the political space they demand. In so doing, they are swelling the ranks of people who, out of frustration or resignation, consider themselves sovereigntists "by default."[9] It is true that Quebecers are weary of effete, sectarian constitutional squabbling, but this in no way means that they are unwilling to think about their political future; they have simply undertaken to articulate their identity outside the stultifying confines of a sterile, old-hat debate. Since politics has not yet shown that it can meet the challenge of contemporary identity indeterminacy, Quebecers have resorted to self-interpretation as a way of understanding the full complexity of their being.[10] Thus this introspection about identity need not be likened to the ontological angst of a people who refuse to pass into History.

Identity in Quebec, at the international as well as the federal level, is therefore problematic. But a situation is made explicit as a result of an awareness of its problematic status. Since individuals and peoples are guided in their daily lives by a certain background comprehension of their situation, it is only when that comprehension becomes inoperative that the situation must be explained and articulated.[11] As we know, the Quebec identity – a perpetual source of concern – has never been able to do without this reflective, inward-looking, objectifying gaze. Still, the intensity of this self-examination has built in recent years. And this phenomenon is not reserved to small, supposedly weak and insecure nations. Even the great powers, such as France and the United States, once thought to be immune to adolescent soul-searching, can no longer abstain from problematizing their identity.

For some, the global pluri-disciplinary interest in the problematics of identity is only an intellectual fad perpetuated by writers who need to prove their own relevance in a pragmatic, utilitarian, calculating world. In the bustle of daily life, with practical considerations constantly in the foreground, who has time to really care about the interpretation of their individual or collective identity? In this period of late modernity when, for example, globalization is leaving a rapidly growing number of people to their own devices, are there not more pressing practical and theoretical issues for our university intellectuals to consider?

For others, and I count myself among them, identity as a concept is being theorized and interrogated with such enthusiasm because it is intrinsically linked to the incessant tribulations of modernity. Identity itself, Zygmunt Bauman and Charles Taylor suggest,[12] is a modern invention; and modernity (of whatever kind, be it "outmoded," "late," or "radicalized") is always fluctuating, being reconstructed, mutating, and, *eo ipso*, shaking up the traditional referents of identity. Nation, gender, class, political affiliation, tradition – the paradigmatic identity codes are increasingly unable to serve as exhaustive, all-structuring frames of reference. It has become virtually impossible to grasp the complexity of identities with reference to only one of their sources. This is what underlies the intense questioning of identity, the need for individuals to rethink their representations of themselves and their culture.

If one accepts the idea that human beings are not atoms, existing prior to and as the building blocks of society, but rather, social animals who self-actualize within complex webs of intersubjective relations, it should come as no surprise that collective identities are constantly being interpreted in diverse ways. Identity is not an objective, natural condition; it is better understood as a narrative project or a "persuasive fiction."[13] Thus the definition of an identity (whether individual or collective) cannot be kept separate from its narration, its articulation within narratives of varying degrees of coherence. Nation and narration, as the historian Jocelyn Létourneau and the post-colonialist theorist Homi Bhabha remind us, are inextricably linked. The sociologist Fernand Dumont is therefore correct when he asserts that collective identities emerge out of the mingling of identity representations with social practices; thus the contours of a nation cannot be discerned if the incessant work of its interpreters is overlooked.[14]

If nationality no longer provides the overarching identity horizon within which the other aspects of a person's life can be constructed, this does not mean that it has been eclipsed or supplanted as a component of identity; rather, nationality has been "detranscendentalized," that is, placed on an equal footing with other sources of identity (sexuality, gender, generational positioning, spirituality, profession, ethnicity, and so on). In the world of today, it is up to active subjects, not theorists, to order and define the importance they assign to the different aspects of their identity. The nation has been desacralized, reconfigured,[15] and it therefore needs to be reconceptualized. But apologies for cosmopolitanism notwithstanding, the nation as an identity horizon did not dissolve; it remains for many a fundamental source of identity. Considering attempts to understand nationality as futile is tantamount to mocking the desire to understand oneself as a human being. Those theorists who have applied themselves to circumscribing the fluctuating bounds of the nation – where "nation" is defined as a discursive space – have learned that there is no hermetic boundary between representation and reality; that, on the contrary, representation is part and parcel of reality. And so their work is seen to be much more than an abstract project taking place within the safe, comfortable quarters of the academic ivory tower.

Introduction

Fernand Dumont reminds us that "we are still groping towards a new figure of ourselves."[16] If so, then anyone who devotes her or himself to the task of interpreting a given national or collective identity may, in addition to describing its parameters, propose alternative conceptions of it. As the philosopher Michel Seymour suggests, conceptualizing the nation "may help us to begin thinking about what we want to be, not just to provide an image of what we already are."[17] Since the universal intellectual belongs to a bygone era,[18] conceptualizers of the nation – those who propound alternative representations and narratives of nationality – are subjects anchored within their object of study, not theoreticians who stand outside the deliberative process and attempt to develop its rules and content. In other words, intellectuals may try to "conduct the conduct" of their fellow citizens in various intersubjective spheres (conforming to the Foucaultian definition of power relations and life in society), rather than legislate or raise their own normative prescriptions to the level of impassable horizons. They recognize that their orientation is specific, not universal, and exemplify their position instead of attempting to impose it.[19] Besides offering my understanding of the dominant interpretations of identity in Quebec, I shall also try to articulate an alternative representation of that identity. The Quebec imagination is saturated – besieged – with two dominant representations of identity, in their different shades and variants: the melancholy nationalist discourse, at times sorrowful and resigned, often vehement and seditious; and the anti-nationalist discourse, rationalist and cosmopolitan. Throughout the recent history of Quebec, from the clashes between *Cité libre* and *Parti pris* in the 1960s to the debates sparked by Marc Angenot's articles in *Le Devoir* in the summer of 1996, these two discourses have persistently gone head to head and regrouped, ultimately coming to regard each other as both mutually limiting and exhaustive of society's political space.

This perennial clash of ideologies has the merit of having helped to elucidate the vexed relationship between nationalism and liberalism; however, it has created the illusion that Quebec identity representations are limited to melancholy nationalism as an outgrowth of a purportedly ingrained cultural fatigue, on the one hand, and cosmopolitan individualism, on the other. The potentialities of identity in Quebec have somehow been squeezed into two large, hermetic, mutually exclusive categories. It is not my intention to challenge the legitimacy of these two discourses but, rather, to question this compression of our identity horizons. Thought and knowledge, says Foucault, can help us to "free ourselves from ourselves," to *become other*, to widen our identity panorama. In this essay I shall explore various ways of "going beyond" our paradigmatic and apparently insurmountable identity narratives. For philosophy can be viewed as "the displacement and transformation of frameworks of thinking, the changing of received values and all the work that has been done to think otherwise, to do something else, to become other than what one is."[20] While the nationalist poet Gaston Miron was impelled by the desire to "create the imagination of a country," I shall pursue the more modest goal of challenging an overly restrictive collective imagination with new possibilities.[21] In other words, I shall attempt to "oxygenate" a discussion that seems at times to be hardly more than a constant reiteration of identical positions. My objective is to take part in a decompartmentalization of the collective imagination and a conversion of our ways of seeing; and in this I am keenly aware of my own limitations.

It is common for authors to exaggerate the novelty and originality of what they write.[22] Be it said that I am certainly not the first to attempt to pluralize our representations of ourselves and our possible political futures. On the contrary, I am working within an established interpretive tradition, one to which I seek to make a contribution. Moreover, it is convenient for writers to blow the importance, the centrality, of their targets out of proportion. Alain Dubuc, for example, in his series of *La Presse* editorials, greatly amplifies and dramatizes the influence of what he calls the "sacred cows of our political thought," in order to put into relief the force and radicalness of his own views about Quebec. He writes that our "obsession" with the national question "leads us to withdraw complacently into ourselves. Prisoners of the past, we are missing out on modernity and limiting our interaction with the world."[23] The least that can be said is that it is difficult to locate this "we" evoked by Dubuc to represent Quebec; he seems to be confusing "Quebec" with a particular discourse about it.

And from a comparative standpoint, no analyses seem more baseless to me than those that portray Quebec as a society captive to its past, incapable of confronting the challenges of modernity, paralyzed by intercommunity tensions. Although I do see the tenacious nationalist/anti-nationalist opposition in Quebec as constricting both our imagination and our political possibilities, I do not think that it overdetermines our societal dynamics. There is nothing backward about the way that diversity is accommodated in Quebec, and for some years now, innovative writings about identity have been increasingly free of nationalist and anti-nationalist dogma. What is more – at least if one subscribes to the synopsis offered by Jean-François Lisée in his recent book – there is in fact no indication that contemporary Quebec is putting obstacles in its path to modernity or limiting its interaction with the world.[24] On the contrary, Lisée thinks that what is threatening the cultural, social, and economic dynamism of Quebec is its demographic and political incapacity to withstand an emboldened and resolutely interventionist federal government.

This essay on the hazy, evanescent boundaries of identity in Quebec is not a history book. It is not my place to judge the historical validity of the various narratives that have been constructed about the Quebec experience during the last forty years. For me, the value of these narratives as historiography is less important than their durability in the minds of the nation's interpreters. One of the fundamental themes of this book is indeed that of atavism, which I define for my purposes here as the process of appropriation/translation whereby various contemporary intellectuals have reiterated and rearticulated certain perspectives that originated in the 1950s and 1960s. Nor am I writing a history of ideas or a sociology of intellectuals, even if an exploration of the works of those who have narrated the Quebec nation since the years preceding the Quiet Revolution obliges me to use some of the techniques of those disciplines.[25] Instead, I shall strive to take part in what Foucault called a "critical ontology of ourselves." This mode of critical reflection on the present, more an attitude than a method or a system, aims to unearth and exhibit what is contingent and arbitrary within what is taken to be necessary and absolute. Critical (and genealogical) ontology may thereby enable us to venture, modestly and laboriously, beyond the most ingrained images of ourselves. "I shall thus characterize the philosophical ethos appropriate to the critical ontology of ourselves," writes Foucault, "as a historico-practical test of the limits that we may go beyond, and thus as work carried out by ourselves upon ourselves as free beings."[26] Clearly, this problematization of

Introduction

what we are is always partial, limited by the set of imaginable options within a given space and time (we can never fully free ourselves from the interpretive frameworks that have preceded us, which both constrain and stimulate new interpretations) and, in consequence, always in need of being begun again. This essay, then, is intended as a contribution to the incessant interpretive work on ourselves as a distinct society in North America.

In this effort I shall explore, assess, and to some extent deconstruct certain of the principal representations of Quebec-ness. This process will oblige me to criticize – at times severely – the work of highly respected and respectable interpreters, from Hubert Aquin to Jean Larose, from the *Cité libre* writers of the past to Jean-Pierre Derriennic today. It is not an easy task, especially for a newcomer, to take issue with the paradigmatic interpretations of identity in Quebec. Though acerbic, scathing debate is in fashion, I have no interest in trading polemical blows with those who have devoted a great deal of energy to rendering identity in Quebec somewhat more intelligible and to proposing alternative conceptions. As Foucault suggests, the polemicist's interlocutor is not "a partner in search for the truth but an adversary, an enemy who is wrong, who is harmful, and whose very existence constitutes a threat."[27] The opposite of polemics, which is fuelled by dogma and closed-minded, static thinking, is "reciprocal elucidation," in which the interlocutors speak in their own terms but recognize the legitimacy of the adverse point of view. Each consents to put his or her own positions into play in light of how the others view the matter. Reciprocal elucidation, for the philosopher James Tully, is always relative, partial, contextual, precarious, and therefore subject to perpetual reconstruction. It is more a sketch, in the Wittgensteinian sense, than it is an exhaustive theory.[28] It involves neither the dogmatic repetition of unshakeable convictions nor the passive, uncritical concession to opposing arguments, but an agonistic encounter of diverging and overlapping ideas. Contrary to Habermasian discourse ethics, it is not at all assumed in the serious, arduous game of reciprocal elucidation that "the force of the better argument" will ultimately sway all the participants.

And at any rate, despite my profound disagreement with certain of their arguments, I could not engage in polemics with the likes of Fernand Dumont or Régine Robin (to name but two); to do so would be to treat them as illegitimate adversaries. For their irrefutable demonstration that the humanities and social sciences in Quebec can aspire to excellence, they deserve much better than to be dragged into the polemical gutter.

There exists in Quebec a whole discourse on the supposed indifference of young Quebecers to social and political issues. Many baby boomers have made their youth in the 1960s, taken up with student demonstrations and revolutionary strategizing, into a kind of benchmark for social and political involvement, a regulative ideal; and with varying degrees of subtlety, they now reproach young people for their political passivity. It is claimed that committed youth are the important party missing from contemporary socio-political debate. Whether caught up in the quest for individual success or given over to idle, self-satisfied hedonism, young Quebecers – it is claimed – have deserted the public square and withdrawn into private life. And when young people do succeed in making themselves heard, they tend to be taken to task for their lack of critical judgment, their conformism, or their inability to make novel yet realistic contributions to society. Between apathy and conformism, there is precious little room for young committed Quebecers to exercise their freedom.

Introduction

As an antithesis to this moralistic discourse (which largely ignores the context in which young people today must define themselves), many youth have come to be convinced that their future has been foreclosed on, that a dead end is all it has in store for them.[29] Central to this reasoning is the idea that the society built by the Quiet Revolutionaries was custom-designed to suit their own needs and, as a result, was unable to accommodate the generations that followed. This structurally truncated, skewed society would inevitably push anything different – that is, young people and their projects for social transformation – to the margins. A good part of Quebec youth is quite at one with this discourse on the alleged sacrifice of an entire generation, and so the praxis of youth movements has largely become limited to systematic opposition, to generalized denunciation and demonization of the Quiet Revolutionaries and the sweeping social reforms they effected. The baby boomer becomes the Other, the ontologically different, in opposition to which youth must define and uphold an imperiled identity.

My work here is an attempt to navigate the rough waters created by these two discourses, each of them excessive, yet each in its way legitimate. It is important, as a young person, to critique both the institutional and the symbolic structures which some baby boomers have internalized to such an extent that they are unable to think critically about them. But if one is to put up resistance to a kind of defeatism, it is just as important to show young people that they are not out of the game; there are still ways for them to make themselves heard, to participate in forging the Quebec of the present day. Polymorphous and plural, Quebec youth must take part in building the political institutions and creating the imagination of a nation for which they will be responsible in the years to come. Obviously, mine is just one voice among many; the time is past when intellectuals could set themselves up as a representative conscience. No one can claim to speak in the name of all of today's young Quebec intellectuals.

Finally, I should note that twenty-six is a young age at which to write words in stone. The exercise of thinking is a peculiar ascetic discipline; only time, diligence, rigour, and humility provide any assurance of arriving at a mature, nuanced, innovative body of thought. These characteristics are somewhat alien to the young person, who watches her or his reflective and creative capacities fluctuate as a function of day-to-day efforts. But philosophy and social and political thought are slowly freeing themselves from their sterile propensity to form definitive systems or theories. Primarily thanks to the contributions of thinkers such as Nietzsche, Wittgenstein, Arendt, Foucault, and, among our contemporaries, Taylor and Tully, philosophy appears to be taking a "practical turn," and philosophical work increasingly emerges in the form of explorations, openings, or sketches that are in perpetual need of revision, correction, and amendment. It is my hope that this essay on the shifting horizons of identity in Quebec will be read in that spirit.

1

Cultural Fatigue and Arrested Development: The Melancholy Nationalists

> Culturally fatigued and weary, French Canada, for a long time now has been going through an endless winter; every time the sun breaks through the ceiling of cloud that has obliterated the heavens, in spite of our weakness, our sickness and disillusionment, we start hoping for spring again.
>
> Hubert Aquin

There exists in Quebec a whole discourse about the fragility, the precariousness, the tragic existence, the fatigue, the modesty, the phillistinism, the mediocrity, the immaturity, and the indecision of the Québécois people. Those who intone this sombre national chant are drinking from a stream with many confluents. By searching a little and by adopting a certain relationship to the past, one can indeed find in the genesis of Quebec society, as well as in its recent history, the fuel for a major depression – or more precisely, a case of collective melancholia. In Freud's terms, melancholia is experienced as a kind of mourning whose sources elude us, which we cannot ascribe to a specific, identifiable loss.[1] That is, melancholia is an elusive, diffuse, latent feeling of grief. From generation to generation, Quebec intellectuals and writers have attempted to follow the thread of this melancholia, in the belief that they can work back to the origins of Quebec's modern-day ills. The causes of our mourning are variously asserted to be the defeat on the Plains of Abraham and the British Conquest, the abandonment of New France by the motherland, the conqueror's domination and the persistent threats of assimilation (of which the Durham Report was the most glaring manifestation), the repeated failures to refound the country (1837–38, 1980, 1995), the constitutional "humiliation" of Quebec (unilateral repatriation of the Constitution in 1982, failure of Meech Lake in 1990), U.S. economic and cultural neo-imperialism, and the North American and global hegemony of the English language. The thinkers who have probed the past for an explanation of the allegedly morose mindset of the Québécois all share a characteristic relationship to history. They implicitly or explicitly embrace the postulate that certain traumatic events in our history have been repressed and internalized within the Québécois collective unconscious. For these "melancholy writers," as I shall term them, following Jocelyn Létourneau's intuition,[2] these events have come to alter the self-consciousness of the Québécois.[3] They have become second nature, a spectre haunting "this little people" of the Americas by structuring its ethos. The trauma is repeated (unconsciously) in every cowardly act of the community, in every missed rendezvous with History; and this phenomenon explains Quebec's difficulties in coming to maturity, its arrested development. The national imagination, in historian and sociologist Gérard Bouchard's expression, feeds on "depressive myths."[4] To emerge from its cultural torpor, say these narrators, Quebec must be reconciled with its past by accepting and appropriating a history strewn with pitfalls and defeats. Only then will it be able to *live* rather than merely *survive*. To use the sporadically recurring metaphors, it is through such a reconciliation that a Quebec in mourning might finally emerge from the *childhood, winter, hibernation, obscurity,* or *darkness* that has characterized its historical process until now. In other words, if we wish to exorcise a past that is murdering the present, then we must fulfill a duty of remembrance and acceptance of this grievous history.

These nationalist authors also share the idea that through a meticulous, systematic examination of Quebec history, it is possible to get at the essence or substance of the Québécois identity;[5] they are, in some sense, seeking after a lost authenticity. To be sure, this does not imply that they agree about the substance of that identity. From the colonized individual who is unconscious of his or her subjection to the Franco- or French-speaking American to the sovereigntist, the reification of the Québécois identity has taken many forms. But since the geopolitical context means that the survival of the Quebec nation can never be taken for granted, the possibility of defining and delimiting Québécois authenticity becomes a necessity. In effect, what these authors are arguing is this: What is the good of struggling to preserve and promote a culture if you are unable to say what makes it special and original? It follows that the Québécois identity must be objectified in order to be defended and promoted. However, as I shall attempt to show in chapter 4, this syllogism is based on a dated and inoperative conception of authenticity.

Yet the melancholy discourse on the ingrained cultural lethargy of the Québécois is not monolithic. Nothing could be more absurd than to lump together the different narrations of the Québécois identity that I shall examine in this chapter into an undifferentiated whole. There are as many differences, even antinomies, as there are similarities among the discourses of Hubert Aquin, Pierre Vallières, Christian Dufour, and Jean Larose (to name but a few). The vague melancholy that seems to unite the authors examined here takes many forms in their writings: pity, protection, empathy, contempt, resignation (flight, exile, withdrawal, radical individualism), activism (consciousness-raising, calls to action or even to violence), demonization of the Other, and so on. In order to elucidate the similarities and differences among the melancholy writers, I shall make a non-exhaustive analysis of their discourse, whose tone ranges from despondency to outrage at the Québécois identity condition, past and present. My intention here is not to define the essence of this interpretive tradition but to detect "family resemblances." In short, I will produce a selective iconography of the field of Quebec identity studies. It would be practically impossible to conduct a complete review of this vast literary and scientific corpus without making it one's sole object of research. For that reason, I have selected the writers whom I see as most representative in the recent history of Quebec. As well, this incursion into the national/melancholy social discourse is not intended as a mere exegetic exercise. My goal is to show the indelibility of this characteristic variety of self-representation in Quebec and, in particular, to discern how it has been reprised and expressed by contemporary writers in the melancholy tradition.

FROM THE MONTREAL SCHOOL TO DUMONT: THE EFFECTS OF THE CONQUEST

In reading Fernand Dumont's *Genèse de la société québécoise*, one rapidly becomes aware of the persistence, throughout Quebec's history, of a discourse in which the "Canadiens," the "French Canadians," or the "Québécois," as they have been called at different times, are a defeated, conquered, annexed, and dominated people. Behind this "objective" condition may be glimpsed the image of French-speaking Quebecers as a brave, hardy, and modest people, but also an ignorant and backward one; a people chilly to the idea of progress, if otherwise cold-tolerant – since their natural habitat is the "winter" of *survivance* ("subsistence"; see appendix B). Paul-Émile Borduas, in his famous manifesto *Refus global*, referred to the French Canadians as a "little people, huddled to the skirts of a priesthood viewed as sole trustee of faith, knowledge, truth and national wealth, shielded from the broader evolution of thought as too risky and dangerous, and educated misguidedly, if without ill intent, in distortions of the facts of history, when complete ignorance was impracticable."[6] Borduas's cry yearned, among other things, for French Canadians to shake off the cultural oppression that "the unhappiest among us stifle quietly within, in shame and in terror of being overwhelmed."

From violent and flamboyant calls for decolonization to more subtle enterprises of collective psychoanalysis, many avenues have been explored by those who have reflected on the effects of the British colonization. Taking for granted the abnormality of the political status and psychological profile of the French-speaking Quebecers, a number of authors have plumbed the past for the sources of these perceived collective pathologies in an attempt to contribute to the normalization of their society. As of the late 1940s, the Montreal school of historical writing, whose principal members were Guy Frégault, Maurice Séguin, and Michel Brunet, attempted to show that "Quebecers had never entirely recovered from the Conquest" of 1760.[7] The British conquest was asserted by these former disciples of Lionel Groulx to be the cataclysmic episode in the history of Quebec, the event that conditioned the subsequent fate of Canada's francophones and whose aftershocks were still being felt in the Quebec of the 1950s and 1960s. The depiction of the Conquest as a founding trauma finds its most striking example in these apocalyptic lines written by Séguin: "It is possible to judge the Anglo-American conquest and the change of empire as a major disaster in the history of French Canada. It was a catastrophe that tore this young colony out of its protective, nurturing environment, impairing its organization as a society and a budding nation, condemning it to annexation, to political and economic subordination."[8]

The verdict is unequivocal: New France was a society preparing to step over the threshold of political, economic, and cultural normality, but annexation to the British Empire set in motion a long process of disorganization and destructuring of French Canada, whose people, argues Frégault, were "broken" by this process.[9] Together, Brunet, Frégault, and Séguin painted the portrait of a French-Canadian society cast in the mould of the other colonial societies of the Americas. As Frégault wrote, "until 1760, the outlook for French America looked similar to that of British America."[10] Only the seismic shock caused by the Conquest could have derailed a people moving steadily toward political normality. Unlike the Université Laval historians, who blamed the francophones themselves for their cultural, economic, and political anomie, historians of the Montreal school "blame[d] it on others – most notably, the English speakers who had conquered Quebec in the eighteenth century and whose descendants still dominated the scene."[11]

In short, the Conquest was claimed to represent a hiatus in the history of Quebec, giving rise to the long purgatory of *survivance*. Since economic, cultural, and political emancipation was structurally impeded by the English occupation, the French Canadians could hope for no better than to subsist; they clung to certain practices and institutions inherited from the French regime, in an attempt to stave off the threat of assimilation as long they could. The choice was clear: survive or perish. For the Montreal school, the tragic existence of the francophones was epitomized by this perpetual dilemma of subsistence or assimilation.

A number of scholars concur that the sources of Québécois neo-nationalism are to be found in the writings of the Montreal school. Brunet, Frégault, and Séguin, having broken with the more conservative clerical nationalism of Groulx, laid the foundations for an ideology of "affirmationism" that has constantly been renewed since then.[12] Unquestionably, these historians did much to shape the minds of an entire generation of Quebec nationalists, who, following Séguin, continue to wonder how it will be possible to "rectify two centuries of history."[13] Convinced of the abnormality of the Québécois identity condition, past and present, the heirs of the Montreal school believe that rectifying our past is the biggest challenge in our history. For them, the path that this rectification must take is already marked out: it is a matter of facing up to our status as a conquered, dominated people, and embarking on a process of decolonization which, two centuries later, is still a work-in-progress.

Hubert Aquin and Parti pris:
French-Canadian Cultural Fatigue

Despite what the prefix seems to indicate, "neo-nationalism" in Quebec represents a tradition of fundamentally discouraged, fatigued intellectuals. The neo-nationalists, to borrow the title of a poem by Gérald Godin, one of their most worthy representatives, are suffering from "homesickness" (*mal au pays*). Their melancholia was already palpable in the somewhat morose, resigned tone of the historians of the Montreal school, but one feels its full intensity in the sorrow and disillusionment of Hubert Aquin, whose personal mission was to articulate, to name, this collective depression. His essay "The Cultural Fatigue of French Canada" is unquestionably one of the founding documents of Québécois melancholy nationalism.

In this reply to an essay by Pierre Trudeau published in *Cité libre*, Aquin undertook to describe the Québécois identity condition at the start of the 1960s.[14] In the image of the melancholy nationalists who followed and preceded him, he considered the historical subjugation of the French Canadians to ensue from their two-century-old status as a minority group. The francophones, he asserted, have developed a set of pathological traits typically found in individuals suffering from powerful inferiority complexes and low self-esteem. This quiet, mundane alienation – nonetheless symptomatic of the whole culture's inertia – underlies what he refers to as the "cultural fatigue of French Canada." For Aquin, the correlation between the neurotic condition he diagnoses in his contemporaries and the persistence of minority-group status is beyond debate: "Is it necessary, in this context, to catalogue all the psychological implications caused by the awareness of this minority position: self-punishment, masochism, a sense of unworthiness, 'depression,' the lack of enthusiasm and vigour – all the underlying reactions to dispossession that anthropologists refer to as 'cultural fatigue'? French Canada is in a state of cultural fatigue and, because it is invariably tired, it becomes tiresome."[15]

This "difficulty of being" evinced by French Canadians is claimed to be the long-term consequence of the constant but subtle subordination of which they have been victims since the end of the French regime. Aquin goes as far as to view the French-Canadian culture as "depressive," implicitly transposing a heuristic category designed for the analysis of the individual psyche to the study of communities. He affirms that the "French-Canadian culture shows all the symptoms of extreme fatigue, wanting both rest and strength at the same time, desiring both existential intensity and suicide, seeking both independence and dependency."[16] This toing and froing between the individual and the collective conscience is, in fact, a characteristic feature of Aquin's thought.[17] He despairs, "I myself am one of these 'typical' men, lost, unsettled, tired of my atavistic identity and yet condemned to it."[18] In the same vein, the protagonist of his novel *Next Episode* does not hesitate to project his personal tribulations onto the historical being and becoming of the French Canadians. History and biography interweave, provoking a paralyzing feeling of revolt and impotence in both Aquin and his fictional character: "I am the fragmented symbol of Quebec's revolution, its fractured reflection and its suicidal incarnation ... To commit suicide everywhere, with no respite – that is my mission. Within myself, explosive and depressed, an entire nation grovels historically and recounts its lost childhood in bursts of stammered words and scriptural raving, and then, under the dark shock of lucidity, suddenly begins to weep at the enormity of the disaster, at the nearly sublime scope of its failure. There comes a time, after two centuries of conquest and thirty-four years of confusional sorrow, when one no longer has the strength to go beyond the appalling vision."[19]

Mired in a fatigued, dying culture, Aquin's French-Canadians oscillate between their desire for revolution and for collective suicide. But despite the shadowland it inhabits, French-Canadian culture, torn between a life instinct and a death instinct, can descry the glow of redemption in the distance. Thus do resignation and activism compose the explosive depression of Aquin and his compatriots. On the one hand, Aquin the essayist argues that "English Canada ... may well still get the better of our *cultural fatigue*, which is very great,"[20] and Aquin the novelist has his hero "about to succumb to historical fatigue";[21] on the other, calls to revolution and emancipation from a debilitating condition are never far off, indicating that he thinks French-Canadian culture is not entirely buried under the weight of history.[22] The conquered ones have "carved out a tiny place between death and resurrection."[23]

For Aquin and his successors in the melancholy tradition, the atavistic nature of the Québécois identity is not in question. The ingrained fatigue he diagnoses is said to be transmitted from generation to generation, in different guises but ontologically unaltered. Those who claim not to feel the effects of these historical injuries are guilty, he argues, of either bad faith or false consciousness. As we shall see later, this unperceived atavism is asserted to be the main stumbling block to the transformation of the Québécois collective consciousness, a transformation insistently called for by the melancholy nationalists since the 1960s.

Even before the publication in 1962 of Aquin's seminal essay in *Liberté*, one could find in the poems of Gaston Miron a forlorn, dying, yet vindictive "we"; indeed, the same bipolar structure characterizes Miron's verse as Aquin's prose. When we read the poem cycle *The Agonized Life*, for example, his view of how the French Canadians have been victimized by profound historical conditioning comes across with great force. Yet just when readers are overcome with lassitude and discouragement, Miron inflames them by pointing the way to a collective escape from alienation:

The Melancholy Nationalists

Now I see how we are in want in this century
I see our inferiority and within each of us I grieve
Today amid the whispering is this square
I hear the animal turning in our tracks
I hear in our resinous subconscious
a rage now rising in a whirlwind of felled trees[24]

In some of his essays, Miron attempts to flush out the multiple and insidious manifestations of the "colonial phenomenon" in Quebec, chiefly in its spoken language. The linguistic alienation of the francophone is presented as in some sense an epiphenomenon of a deeper inability to confront alterity – what Miron calls "the French-Canadian neurosis vis-à-vis the Other."[25] The degrading, humiliating gaze of the Anglo-Canadian other has laid waste to the francophones' self-image, and so the task facing the latter is to "acknowledge" their condition as a colonized people and then to subvert it by turning it into a positive affirmation. On this acceptance, according to Miron (following the historians of the Montreal school), depends "the emergence of authenticity," an authenticity deeply buried under decades of linguistic, cultural, political, and economic subordination.[26]

The theme of Quebec's awakening from a long, dogmatic slumber is most sharply delineated in the writings of Aquin, Miron, Godin, and other contributors to *Liberté* and *Parti pris*. This emancipation is presented at once as a coming to awareness, an articulation of the collective psychological conditioning at the root of the Québécois' shame and self contempt, and a release from this psychological condition (by means of a violent, cathartic break). As André-J. Bélanger rightly notes, this dialectic is fundamental to the approach taken by the early *Parti pris* contributors. Aligning themselves with the neo-nationalist historical narrative, they "held the Conquest of 1760 accountable for the present predicament of the

Québécois."[27] In tune with an intellectual epoch in which the Parisian psychoanalytic tradition held great influence over many intellectuals, *Parti pris* contributors such as Pierre Maheu and Paul Chamberland argued that the "psychoanalytic observation of a Québécois pathology"[28] (the dislocation of consciousness caused by the subtle domination of the colonizer) and the exploration of the collective unconscious are prerequisites for any political and cultural emancipation. The founding members of *Parti pris* wanted to uncover and exhibit the occupation of the Québécois mind by the Other. This, they argued, enabled the conqueror to determine and fashion the Québécois self-image according to his own values and interests, thus saddling francophones with endemic and pervasive feelings of shame and contempt to which they have been unable to imagine an alternative. "For *Parti pris*," Bélanger opines, "the Other's great feat was surely to cause us to repress the normal resentment we should have nurtured against him, instead turning it against ourselves in the form of culpability, that is, self-hatred." [29] Consequently, the priority of the early *Parti pris* contributors was to spur the Québécois people on to a new consciousness, which they saw as the precursor to a genuine national liberation movement. Having assimilated Marx's meditations on the consequences of capitalist exploitation and Frantz Fanon's on the effects of colonialism, the *Parti pris* writers agreed with the latter that it is impossible for the colonized person to "go forward resolutely unless he first realizes the extent of his estrangement" (from his or her own people).[30]

The theoretical heritage of psychoanalysis was not, however, their only ideological influence. The *Parti pris* members could not stop at a thoughtful statement of the francophones' socio-cultural neurosis, for they were also versed in Marxism and anti-colonialism, and thus were driven by a desire to develop a praxis that could break the chains of national alienation. In the era of African decolonization and Che Guevara, the Québécois anti-colonial nationalists inevitably saw the relevance to their own situation of an international conjuncture marked by the fall of European imperialism.[31] However, even if they concurred on the therapeutic virtues and the absolute necessity of a sharp break with the Anglo-Canadian other, not all of them saw violence as a necessary phase. *Parti pris*'s position on the subject of violence emerged as a composite of its main contributors' shifting views. Some endorsed Aquin's Sartrean position to the effect that "there is no possible shortcut from a collectively felt inferiority to equal-to-equal collaboration," while others felt that it was tactically imprudent and inadvisable to resort to force as a means of awakening francophones to their condition.[32] In general, propaganda, consciousness-raising, legal action, clandestine resistance, and even parliamentarianism were presented as the most appropriate ways to manifest one's dissidence, while armed struggle seems to have been perceived mainly as a last resort. Despite the relationship between *Parti pris* and the Front de Libération du Québec, the FLQ's ideology in fact represented a radicalization of the journal's stance.

For these writers, the exploration of the Québécois collective psyche, envisaged in some sense as the rectification of the harm suffered over the years, remained the preferred means of arriving at an authentic Québécois "we," a mature people liberated from the subtle domination of the Anglo-Canadian other. Convinced that colonialism is a "thousand-headed hydra" (Fanon), the *Parti pris* writers put an emphasis on uncovering and publicizing the multiple manifestations of the colonial phenomenon in Quebec. For example, Gérald Godin, in his column "Chroniques du colonialisme quotidien," was at great pains to unveil the polymorphous nature of Canadian domination. "At the risk of being thought insane," wrote the politician-poet, "one must be obsessed with rooting out colonialism wherever it is found."[33] In this context, the role of the anti-colonial Québécois intellectual was "to unmask, to decode the quotidian colonial hallucination."[34]

It should be said that denunciation of the colonialist essence of the Canadian federal system was not the exclusive prerogative of *Parti pris*. André D'Allemagne, a founder of the early separatist party Rassemblement pour l'Indépendance Nationale (RIN), thought that the Confederation of 1867, the slow and spasmodic modernization of Quebec in the first half of the twentieth century, and the Quiet Revolution had not in any way changed the fact that the Québécois people remained deeply colonized and alienated. Far from a bygone phenomenon belonging to Quebec's prehistory, colonialism still underlay the mental, political, and economic structures of Quebec society. The political freedom gained in the 1960s was only a sham, a fancy entertained by intellectuals and politicos who had no idea how alienated they really were. In D'Allemagne's estimation, Anglo-Canadian neo-colonialism, by virtue of its insidious and elusive nature, had simply put one over on these elites.

And this outcome was not surprising, according to D'Allemagne, since they were in fact *colonized from the inside*; it was not so much that their hands were tied by anglophone domination, but that their minds were controlled by it. He writes that "occupation by brute force gave way to a kind of psychological conditioning. The colonized people lost spirit and motivation. Their history was extinguished. Henceforth they would exist on the margins; their weary, eked-out subsistence was but a sideshow for the life of the colonizer."[35]

The Melancholy Nationalists

It is the "apparent absence of the colonizer" that makes the Canadian colonial system such a perverse and effective structure of domination. In this respect, D'Allemagne's analysis is not radically different from that of the melancholy nationalists we have examined so far. Earlier, in the historical narration of the Université de Montréal neo-nationalist historians, one could find an analysis of the physical and psychological hardships engendered by colonialism. Yet in 1966, when political and economic affirmationism was omnipresent in the social discourse of Quebec, the portrayal of its society as a colony exploited economically and politically by the Anglo-Canadian majority was more difficult to defend. And so D'Allemagne and others reprised Frégault's diagnosis that the Conquest had signed the death warrant of French-Canadian society by playing up the psychological consequences of the francophones' historical undoing. In his political psychology, D'Allemagne drew heavily on the ideas of the African anti-colonialist intellectuals. He argued that "starting in childhood and throughout their existence, the Québécois are subjected to conditioning that evokes in them all the typical reflexes of the colonized around the world today."[36]

With this inferiority complex ever more firmly embedded in the psyche of the Québécois, our society was claimed to be existing in a state of perpetual and progressive decrepitude, and Canadian colonialism, in the words of D'Allemagne, was "a never-ending genocide."[37] Existential angst, cowardice, conservatism, withdrawal into oneself, and xenophobia were perceived by him as the direct consequences of the Québécois' psychological colonization. Only decolonization and independence, the leitmotifs of the RIN, could catalyze the mental emancipation of each individual francophone.

Pierre Vallières: Between Socio-economic and National Alienation

A nigger's life is no life at all. And all Québécois were (and are) niggers.

Pierre Vallières

Quite clearly, what unites all the different narratives discussed to this point in a sort of metanarrative is a denunciation of the alienation (understood as dispossession or a feeling of "no longer belonging or becoming a stranger to oneself")[38] experienced by the French-Canadian historical being. However, the kind of alienation at issue has almost exclusively been considered *cultural* or *national*, that is, the oppression of the francophones by virtue of their linguistic and cultural minority status. But the *Parti pris* contributors and others were also concerned with the economic subordination and the rampant proletarianization of Quebec society. Francophones' alienation, they felt, was both national and economic in nature;[39] alienation in the Marxist sense of the term was added to the alienation described by Groulx and his successors. The Québécois, according to the anti-colonial nationalists, were structurally confined to both their colonized and their proletarian identities; they were denied access to the means of cultural and economic production. Hence the Québécois revolution desired and theorized by the *Parti pris* contributors had to be both nationalist and socialist.

However, recent commentators disagree in their analysis of the hierarchy of values characteristic of the journal. Andrée Fortin, in her meticulous analysis of Quebec intellectual journals, argues that for *Parti pris*, "nationalism went hand in hand with socialism, political and cultural revolution with economic revolution."[40] In somewhat different terms,

Bélanger evokes the possibility that the *Parti pris* contributors had subordinated socialist revolution to nationalist revolution, the latter being the precondition for the former. Moreover, according to Bélanger, although they made frequent reference to social conditions and socialism, these were greatly undertheorized until much later, when social science–trained intellectuals such as Gilles Bourque and Louis Racine came on the scene. It is in the latter's contributions that "Quebec is truly situated as being on the periphery of capitalist development in North America, where effective control is held by the U.S. monopolies."[41]

Whichever of these interpretations is closer to reality, the hierarchy of national alienation and economic exploitation is abruptly upended in the work of an activist intellectual such as Pierre Vallières, author of the well-known *White Niggers of America* and one-time member of the FLQ. Although he did not ignore the dual nature of Québécois alienation, Vallières always refused to subordinate class struggle to national liberation – whence, for example, his oft-repeated disapproval of a Parti Québécois he considered insufficiently critical of the dictates of Western market economism. For Vallières, the socialist revolution could not be subordinated to national independence because "[American] imperialism is not interested in flags: one flag more or less in no way disturbs its universal system of exploitation of natural resources and cheap labour."[42]

The self and the other in Vallières take a different form from those in the other authors studied: instead of the opposition between French- and English-speaking Canadians, we have the opposition between the (Québécois) proletariat and U.S. economic imperialism; national liberation, in his view, cannot be theorized as taking place within the territorial limits of Quebec. There is also a shift in how the ethical substance of the Québécois is described; Vallières's primary characterization of the francophones is as a source of cheap labour. With the publication of *White Niggers of America*, the figure of the exploited worker takes its place alongside that of the depressive and the (culturally) alienated individual in iconographic representations of Quebec. Francophones are still victims of powerful psychological conditioning that renders illusory the development of an authentic, autonomous identity, but the source of this conditioning is no longer historical domination by the British; it is the working-class "childhood" of the majority of francophones. What Vallières finds "inhuman" in this condition is "the child's powerlessness to resist the conditioning not only of the system itself but of all the frustrations of the life around him, frustrations that are generated by the capitalist organization of society and that contaminate him even before he becomes aware of their existence."[43] From this standpoint, liberating the Québécois, those "born losers," requires an anti-capitalist, anti-imperialist, and anti-colonialist war.

But even though Vallières adds an international and Marxist dimension to the study of Quebec's predicament, he remains inhabited, pervaded, by the melancholia worn in different guises by each new generation of Québécois nationalist intellectuals. Despite an intellectual youth influenced by existentialism and phenomenology, during which he attempted to comprehend the "traditional capacity of the Québécois for resignation" in its multiple phenomenological manifestations and to devise a radical individualist theory of freedom, Vallières kept on hearing the "long sorrowful song of our alienation."[44] "But like all the other Québécois, I too was imprisoned in the land of winter and the great darkness," he recalls on this subject.[45] Winter, darkness, night, obscurity – these are the metaphors punctuating his description of the Québécois condition. Even if he comprehends its source, the Québécois lethargy causes Vallières to succumb at times to a profound bitterness with respect to the people he and others sought to bring out of their caves. In the introduction to his collection *La liberté en friche*, his anger is palpable: "The cultural fatigue of French Canada, which so aroused the indignation of Hubert Aquin, engenders an endless supply of cowardice and mediocrity ... At base, the 'Quiet Revolution' changed nothing ... Like the French Canadians of the past, the Québécois are afraid of freedom."[46] In the image of the melancholy writers as a group, Vallières entertains a relationship that fluctuates between empathy for and discouragement with his homeland, which is a source of both revolutionary exaltation and profound bitterness for him.

This fear of freedom, this cowardly, dangerous ambiguity, this timorous streak in the Québécois psyche are all the targets of Vallières's accusing finger.[47] In fact, consternation at the atavistic cowardliness of the francophones is a trait shared by most of the melancholy writers. As early as 1953, Pierre Vadeboncœur made the following observation in the pages of *Cité libre*: "defeated, too uncertain of our destiny, in the minority, we have acquired the bad habit of refusing to let ourselves be led where our will takes us."[48] Like the others, Vallières postulates that only a violent catharsis can rouse a community drowsy from decades of alienation. Such a catharsis, he argues, can only be provoked by a people's revolution whose effects are those of a "successful collective psychoanalysis."[49]

Fernand Dumont and the (Perpetual) Childhood of Quebec

The desire to subject the Québécois past to a psychoanalytic treatment has never been renounced by the nationalist intellectuals. The writings and political action of Camille Laurin, a former psychiatrist and minister in the PQ government and the father of Bill 101, are exemplary in this regard. Since the consequences of the Conquest are still not acknowledged, assimilated, and sublimated by many Québécois, the exploration of the Québécois collective unconscious, an exploration of those consequences, must be the necessary preliminary step in the development of our autonomy and maturity. Fernand Dumont, though, is without question the Quebec scholar who has articulated this hermeneutic approach to the interpretation of ourselves with the greatest subtlety, nuance, lucidity, and rigour. A contemporary of the authors discussed above, he was the one who gave the greatest substance and depth to this collective psychoanalytic undertaking. He plumbed the very soul of the Québécois for the sources of their historical malaise, their difficulty in accepting their existence as a people. Well versed in history, philosophy, theology, and the various disciplines of the social sciences, Dumont was the best equipped of his contemporaries to take up the impossible task of sounding the collective unconscious of the Québécois people. In his work he confronted what he called the "modest but troubling tragedy" of Quebec.

It would be facile, in reviewing this work, to reduce Dumont's narration of the Québécois identity to an abortive attempt to transpose the categories of individual psychoanalysis to the interpretation of societies and history (which, as the philosopher Serge Cantin rightly points out, was not Dumont's direct intention),[50] and I would be doing him an equal injustice to claim that he had a static – and therefore untenable – vision of the historical formation of Quebec society. As a sociologist, he was attempting to identify and isolate the traits which had been formed by certain collective experiences occurring in the "childhood" of Quebec society, and which remained constant through the perpetual reconfigurations of the Québécois mind. Put another way, one part of Dumont's project was to detect repetition in change. Like his contemporaries and his heirs, he thought he had found the source of this repetition, named "atavism" by the authors I have discussed so far, in the genesis of Quebec society.

In his analysis of the Quebec condition, Dumont took as his starting point the postulate – shared by all the melancholy thinkers – that the Québécois identity is indecisive, ailing, flirting more or less consciously and intensely with the conditions of its own ruin. Thus the urgency and the necessity of working back to the sources of the malaise: "When the collective identity begins to crumble, one is led to return to its genesis, to ask by what process it was imposed in the first place; this seems necessary if one is to arrive at a new awareness of self."[51] Dumont's agenda, then, was to investigate the birth and childhood of the society, highlighting certain stages of its development, so as to lighten the weight of history to whatever extent possible. He sought to cut a path into the "deep layers" of the Québécois past and, in so doing, to gather up the years of alluvial deposits overlying the Québécois self-image. For him, nothing was more important than to examine the alluvia left by history, for he saw them as still structuring the collective possibilities of the French-Canadian nation even in the twentieth century.[52]

According to Dumont, this inchoate psychological trait is the throughline of the French-Canadian/Québécois experience, from the inception of the community to the present day. The origin is the founding and decisive episode, "the crucial moment to which the search for a collective identity refers."[53] But in Dumont's historical narration, the birth of French-Canadian society takes the form of an "abortion," a "failure," an "interruption," or a "trauma." In the gap between the

European utopia of a New France unburdened of the defects of the old one and the feeble and insufficient colonization undertaken to achieve it, a wound still festers. It is here that Dumont situates the birth of the French community in the Americas. He states that, "early on, the projection of the European dream onto New France was interrupted, such that the *origin* looks to us now less like a beginning than an abortion."[54] Even before the Conquest, French-Canadian society was broken, with a wounded self-image and a skewed world view. It was stripped of its illusions and ambitions, a society already in trauma, nestling within the downy utopia that the British would come to occupy. Quebecers would be eternally palliating the effects of this "early childhood trauma" by ideating a utopian future or, in Dumont's words, by the "compensatory work of the imagination."[55]

Although Dumont represents a departure in that he does not see the Conquest as a catastrophic break, it was still, for him, a decisive stage when a troubled, ambiguous, negative self-image was instilled. Though transformed to some degree, his reading of the Conquest as a trauma echoes that of Séguin, Brunet, and Frégault. He too believed that the long, endemic economic and political subjection of Quebec ensued from the change of empire. However, Dumont was "inclined to reprove the historians of the Montreal school for focusing too much of their attention on the event itself, and not enough on its influence on the collective memory, on the inferiority complex still evinced by the francophones of this country, the result of their long submission and the internalization of the self-image mirrored at them by their adversaries."[56] And indeed, in interpreting the genesis of the Québécois identity, he focuses his attention on how the original defeat and annexation affected our historical memory and self-awareness. Like his contemporaries,

Dumont maintains that the internalization of the paternalistic but contemptuous gaze of the Other is the heaviest and most decisive consequence of the anglophone colonization of francophones' self-image. The latter, he asserts, have been observing, scrutinizing, interpreting, and talking about themselves from the standpoint of the conqueror without being much aware of it. Self-image and the presence of the Other have become (con)fused.[57] The discourse of *survivance* was built, according to Dumont, on this very second nature that had become the Other's gaze: "What should be noted in this long apology for *survivance* is less a protest against submission than the slow and subtle appropriation of the image projected by the Other onto the self. Through the incessant repetition of the same arguments to convince the conqueror of the value of a French society's existing, these ultimately become one's own reasons for being."[58]

According to Dumont, the French Canadians will, at critical moments of their existence, be constantly taking refuge in the image of themselves projected by the Other – not only to combat ethnocide but also to find in it "the firmest representation of their identity."[59] In Dumont's narrative, the introjection and appropriation of the occupier's degrading gaze acts as the "rocky substrate," the essence of the French-Canadian and Québécois identity – an essence which, it must be said, is not metaphysical and atemporal but resolutely historical and durably inscribed on the Québécois being. It arises from the accretion of the Other's discourse onto the self. The essence of the Québécois being is found in the slow but perpetual fossilization of a discourse in which the francophone is relegated to the role of subordinate. However, since this discourse is historically constructed, it is subject to being modified or altered. Patient and meticulous archaeological work can unearth these narrative sediments that are firmly layered over the Québécois self-image. That is why, if one wishes to label Dumont an "essentialist," it must be said that his is a historical, relational, and hence temporal essentialism that does not presuppose an immutable, eternal nature.[60] In chapter 4 I shall attempt to show that, if it is perhaps impossible to interpret an identity condition without resort to ontology, it is currently necessary to build up (historical) ontologies that can include multiple authenticities, which do not seek to close themselves off behind hermetic boundaries.

To return to the Dumontian narrative, the appropriation of the image reflected by the Other is asserted to be responsible for the self-contempt and self-hatred that have allegedly stirred within the Quebec francophones since their origins. The "price" of subsistence, for Dumont, is the atavistic, ingrained feeling of inferiority lived and experienced by each new generation of Québécois.[61] This low self-esteem, he asserts, is one of the hallmarks of the French-Canadian people. Dumont had no trouble conceding that, in the 1960s mainly, certain Québécois authors attempted to unearth and explain this self-contempt on which the Québécois identity was based. Thus, he writes, some observers "saw fit to unmask that which we have had such difficulty admitting throughout our history: our self-contempt. No doubt we had appropriated the gaze that the conqueror directed at us, which oscillated between pity for our backwardness and tenderness for our folkloric ways ... A feeling of inferiority being one of our hallmarks, we nurtured it, as one of the ways of practising subsistence. Have we recovered from this illness?"[62] According to Dumont, despite the people's growing awareness of the quasi-hegemonic and constrictive nature of self-contempt in the Québécois mind, it is not certain – far from it – that this chronic inferiority complex is really gone from the Québécois ethos, that we are truly *cured* of this historical disease. Moreover, since an open, confident relationship with difference depends on healthy self-esteem, he claimed (as did Miron) that "the difficulty in confronting other cultures" emanates from this negative self-image.[63]

Dumont never maintains that society simply remained immobile while only the historical scenery changed; still, it is quite evident from his work that he saw our contemporary identity malaise as being rooted in attitudes and ways of being inherited from the past. "A century later," he writes, "the genesis has left us with problems that have yet to find solutions, reflexes that resemble repetitions."[64] On the Dumontian vision of Quebec, Heinz Weinmann has stated that "it is an utterly melancholy vision of the world, of a Quebec born with the death of French Canada, which it has introjected – a Quebec built on the rickety foundations of French Canada."[65] Dumont's diagnosis is clear: despite the Quiet Revolution and the emergence of affirmationism, "the underlying situation has hardly changed at all." Given "the persistence of our mental colonization, our exile in representations that are not really ours," we are still characterized by flight from the past in the compensatory work of dreaming and utopia.[66] In attempting to throw off the chains of the past, the Quiet Revolutionaries reinvigorated their own submission. Dumont writes: "I am tempted to think that, in desiring to free ourselves from ourselves, we have strayed further, through new vicissitudes, down the path of colonialism we have been following since the origins of our community."[67]

This persistent, inexorable mental colonization is manifested, according to Dumont and the majority of the melancholy nationalists, in the political and identity ambiguity characteristic of the Québécois people. This ambiguity is perceived as an abnormality, a congenital deformity, a problem to be solved in order to reach another stage in our collective becoming (maturity). In the work of Dumont, contemporary identity ambiguity must be analyzed with reference to the paradoxical structure of French-Canadian identity in the nineteenth century, in which both the defence of French specificity (i.e., *survivance*) and the demand for political freedoms within the British parliamentary system (constitutional struggles) were integral parts. This contradiction "has never really been overcome since then."[68]

Our contemporary identity, writes Dumont, is "problematic," "confused." So many elements come together in his vision: a birth that took the form of an abortion, a conquest, a multi-dimensional process of subordination, the slow but progressive assimilation of the Other's degrading gaze, a self-image layered with contempt and shame, and our infamous political ambiguity and indecision. Given all this, Dumont could hardly have arrived at a conception of the contemporary Québécois identity as other than idling, procrastinating, dying, saddening. He is basically of one mind with his contemporaries and heirs in believing that a break with political tradition, a new beginning in the form of independence, could catalyze a transformation of the French-Canadian national self-image. With sovereignty, certain struggles ensuing from the Conquest could finally "die quiet deaths," writes Dumont, even as he rejects the totalizing rhetoric of one variety of separatist discourse.[69] Independence, he feels, could provide the foundation for a new discursivity, a new vocabulary of identity, and a new referent for the Québécois in the definition of their collective identity. Thus both regret and hope are palpable when he writes: "There are peoples who can refer in their past to some great founding action: a revolution, a declaration of independence, a resounding departure that keeps alive the certainty of their grandeur. In the genesis of Quebec society, there is no such thing; only an enduring resistance."[70]

As I shall attempt to show below, this fetishization of the foundation colours the imaginations of young intellectuals, such as Daniel Jacques and Marc Chevrier, who are still seeking the conditions of a "solid foundation." While they wait, the melancholy nationalists exhort and anticipate the day when the Québécois will finally add the "courage of freedom" to the "obstinate patience of olden times." Only thus will history begin again to run its course, so that the Québécois can finally emerge from their long and despondent "hibernation."[71]

FROM CANTIN TO LAROSE: VARIATIONS ON THE THEME OF CULTURAL FATIGUE

As I mentioned at the beginning of this chapter, this excursion into the melancholy nationalist social discourse is not a purely exegetic exercise. My purpose in undertaking it is to show how this discourse has taken its place as a dominant trope or representation among Quebec identity theories since the 1950s. From the historians of the Montreal school to Dumont, one can discern the outlines of a pervasive – in fact, omnipresent – melancholy narrative with gloomy and at times thoroughly vengeful overtones. More than four decades separate the work of Dumont and the neo nationalist historians. Is this enough to postulate the persistence of this melancholy narrative approach to identity? Probably not. To make such an assertion, it will be necessary to study the work of contemporary writers to determine their parentage with the authors examined thus far. Of course, until very recently,

Dumont's was still the most subtle, comprehensive version of this overarching collective narrative. But it should be realized that he belonged to the generation of intellectuals who actively took part, as both agents and spectators, in the reconfiguration of Quebec society and identity. He was on hand as the society emerged out of the shadows and into the light (to use a metaphor that is now a standard part of our identity representation repertoire, if not a strictly accurate depiction of history). In order, then, to convincingly demonstrate the transmission and perpetuation of the melancholy nationalist discourse from one generation to the next, it is insufficient to invoke Dumont; for until his death in 1997, he was a contemporary of his intellectual heirs, over whom he towered. I shall therefore show how this discourse has been reclaimed and reworked in the writings of his followers and others. Once the persistence of this discourse is demonstrated, I shall venture to put forward new approaches to the characterization of our identity – and in doing so, I am faithful to the critical ontology of the present that I discussed in my introduction.

Four Contemporary Versions

Of Fernand Dumont's intellectual descendants, it is perhaps the philosopher Serge Cantin who most openly displays his direct lineage. In a collection of essays with the highly revealing title of *Ce pays comme un enfant* (This childlike country), Cantin explores the "atavistic fatigue" of the Québécois. He takes up the heuristic concerns and categories developed by the neo-nationalists, adapting them to the problems and torments of today's society in Quebec. Once again, traits such as cultural fatigue, arrested development, alienation, stagnation, ambiguity, and anemic willpower are adduced as the "hard core" of the Québécois identity condition. Cantin, like his predecessors, wants to psychoanalyze our unhappy consciousness; in fact, he explicitly postulates the existence of a Québécois collective unconscious.[72] Its origins, he writes, are to be found in the pitfalls, "the defeats, the maddening waiting" that have punctuated the history of Quebec since its beginnings. For Cantin, peoples have "inner lives" that unconsciously structure their way of being in the world.[73] The inner life of a people arises out of an inadequately assimilated and acknowledged collective memory; it is a "type of causality" that orients their character and guides their consciousness. Quebec, in this vision, is still afflicted by its "hereditary ills": for example, the "shame" observed by Cantin in the writings of contemporary Quebec intellectuals.[74] The "native alienation" of the people has never been overcome.[75] In short, for him, the dignity of the Québécois is deeply buried under the Plains of Abraham, the symbol of both abandonment by the motherland and annexation to the new empire. In his melancholy narrative, Quebec is "not out of the woods yet."

Cantin's writings on Quebec, especially his moving but depressing correspondence with Jean Bouthillette, often resemble chronicles of a death foretold. With each "collective drama" experienced by the Québécois people, he sees the cultural weariness that is leading Quebec slowly to extinction growing more intense, more draining. The subjectivity of the Québécois, their way of being in the world, today still takes the form of subsistence. The role of the intellectual in this context, he feels, is to shepherd, guide, supervise, and admonish the immature child that is Quebec.[76] Ontologically fragile and insecure, Quebec must be carried like a child to the threshold of maturity; for, left to itself, it has "difficulty becoming an adult, taking charge of its own affairs."[77] Cantin is faithful to his predecessors in suggesting two ways of fostering Quebec's transition toward "self-mastery."

First, he urges his compatriots to reappropriate their language and history, and since they are "children," it is logical that this reappropriation and acceptance take the form of a far-reaching "collective pedagogy."[78] Specifically, he argues that the characteristic Québécois denial of the past results "from what Freud called the 'repetition compulsion,'" in which one is haunted by the memory of one's past defeats and humiliations.[79] Francophones' denial of the past in particular takes the form, allegedly, of a refusal to admit their own status as a colonized people. Cantin argues that this obstinate denial shows signs of a mental colonization far graver and more ingrained than mere physical occupation: "the [Quebec] colonial's inability to recognize himself as being colonized is indicative of a more subtle, insidious, perhaps more profound, and thus less easily eradicable colonization than that of the Algerians or the Vietnamese, for example."[80] The hypothesis of the historical false consciousness of the Québécois, though never explicitly pronounced, is made a postulate. The implication is that only by accepting and appropriating a painful past can Cantin's Quebec put an end to the "unconscious repetition of that past."[81] Like the neo-nationalist intellectuals with whom he makes common cause, he emphasizes the "future of memory, the possibility of turning to the past as a wellspring for meanings until now forgotten, denied, or censured." [82] In this view, liberation depends fundamentally on remembrance.

Secondly, if Quebec society is to stop stumbling at the threshold of autonomy and maturity, Cantin says it must cast off the burden of its "double identity." Here again, the ambiguity, the duality, of the Québécois political subject is deemed responsible for his or her presumed stagnation, and political independence is likened to adulthood. Cantin endorses Dumont's assertion that only "a great political project" can "reconcile" a divided and fragmented national community.[83]

In more acid tones, the critic and professor of literature Louis Cornellier addresses essentially the same themes as Cantin, he too avowing his Dumontian lineage. "The Québécois," he writes, "suffer from acute cultural alienation. In other words, we're a fine bunch of serfs."[84] This cultural alienation, he argues, is so pernicious that it is practically invisible and impalpable. Consequently, "the tragedy of the colonized is that the worse their condition gets, the less their conscious mind is likely to be bothered by it."[85] The corollary of Cornellier's "soft colonization" is the tragic "indifference of its victims."[86] His historical narration has Quebec at the close of the 1960s about to step over the threshold of normality and autonomy. But this passage, which he associates with the decolonization enterprise of the 1960s and 1970s, was short-circuited by Anglo-American cultural imperialism in all its subtle, disparate guises. In a manner reminiscent of Vallières, Cornellier rearticulates the boundaries of the inside and the outside in Quebec culture, maintaining that "we are still colonized, but in a different and more insidious way. Canadian federalism as such is no longer the only obstacle to our emancipation; we now have a worldwide pattern ... in which the identity void is trumpeted as an ideal, so as to make life easier for the steamroller of international Anglo-cultural imperialism and its manifold strategies."[87] In this view, too, the role of the intellectual is to provoke the stirrings of consciousness so cruelly lacking among the Québécois. It is the intellectual's job to turn on the lights, to bring the Québécois out of their caves, where they have grown so accustomed to living in darkness that they can no longer even conceive of light.[88]

The relationships among the themes repeatedly addressed by the melancholy nationalists (repression of a traumatic past, collective amnesia, condemnation of identity ambiguity, arrested or impeded development, independence as a cathartic release of repressed trauma out of the id and into the ego, and so on) are perhaps most clearly elucidated in a brief and vitriolic pamphlet by the philosopher Laurent-Michel Vacher. In his view, the ideological matrix of Quebec separatism in its original and purest form was founded on "a courageous (some would say pessimistic) diagnosis of the ills afflicting Quebec as a consequence of defeat, dependence, and submission – the introjection of the figure of the Other, a collective inferiority complex, a murky, hesitant identity, a relative cultural backwardness, a profound linguistic malaise, the exclusion from modern economic activity and decision-making centres, excessive deference to authority and tradition, etc."[89] In an approach greatly resembling that of the intellectuals discussed so far, Vacher maintains that "for any people that has ever been defeated and dominated, achieving independence becomes a redemptive stage in its history. Beyond the institutional and political manifestations, *it is fundamentally a kind of liberatory psychodrama, a catharsis of rebirth and purification of the collective unconscious.*"[90] Vacher too, then, subscribes to a historical psychoanalysis of the Québécois people.

Since he sees the value and legitimacy of Quebec liberation as being rooted in the desire to cure the malaise inhabiting the "soul," the "identity," of the Québécois people, independence must take the form of a violent, cathartic, redemptive break with a past too painful to bear; it must be a clear and resounding act of self-affirmation. Viewing contemporary politics through this filter, Vacher condemns the sovereignty-associationism propounded by René Lévesque and his disciples (the dominant position within the sovereigntist movement today) as being timorous and convoluted. Such a proposal would only fortify the "internalization of ambiguity" that has afflicted the Québécois people since birth. The associationist variant of the sovereigntist project is a sham, not a release or an outlet, and its "psychohistorical electroshock" value is nil.[91] Thus Vacher calls sovereignty-association a "schizoid variant of neo-federalist autonomism disguised as drawing-room nationalism," a "comfortable scam," an "unsavoury diversionary tactic," a "bastard half-measure."[92] Those who believe in the "historical necessity" of independence but support sovereignty-association are, he thinks, engaging in an utter, performative contradiction.

Vacher too believes that the Québécois are resorting to the compensatory work of the imagination to deny or paper over an intolerable reality. The amnesiac sovereigntists, he contends, are in denial about the failed referenda and are now clinging to the fantasy that Quebec is already a country, that "the Québécois people are 'virtually' sovereign, the catharsis of national affirmation basically behind us."[93] This will to believe in "liberation" as a *fait accompli* evidences a "neurotic false-consciousness," which is in turn the product of an "internally indecisive, ambivalent, split psyche stemming from the ancestral domination." And so like the other theorists, Vacher takes for granted that the Québécois, particularly the sovereigntists, are but the dupes of their own unconscious. The soul of the Québécois is a puppet, and History pulls the strings.

By now it should be obvious that the collective repression of an intolerable past is a hypothesis that has seduced the majority of the melancholy nationalist intellectuals of the last forty years. Instead of opening their eyes and letting the tears flow, the Québécois, it appears, would prefer to keep them closed but nice and dry.[94] They are still alleged to be using repression as a means of alleviating the intense suffering that remembrance would provoke. Although hard to prove, this hypothesis of the collective unconscious has the advantage of pinpointing the source of the "crisis of memory"; moreover, it offers an explanation for what is called our congenital ambiguity, indecision, and lack of resolve.

Coming at this subject from a similar angle, the political scientist Christian Dufour, too, considers repressed trauma to be an appropriate way of describing the derelict condition arising from abandonment and the Conquest. He suggests that the political protagonism of the Quebec francophones is forever marked by the aftershocks of this original seismic event. Chased out of the conscious collective mind, the emotional injuries of the past have nonetheless infiltrated the Québécois psyche: "For Quebecers are still very much affected by the aftermath of the abandonment/conquest they experienced in the 18th century, which remains buried in their collective subconscious."[95] Dufour claims that the abandonment and Conquest have never been grieved, accepted, or transcended, and that consequently, the perpetual repetition of this original hurt constitutes the essence of the contemporary Québécois (and Canadian) identity. Despite the apparent catharsis represented by the Quiet Revolution, the identity of today's Québécois, like that of the French Canadians of the past, remains overdetermined by repressed trauma. The Canadiens, the French Canadians, the Québécois, in their successive incarnations, share a metahistorical identity condition without being fully aware of it: "When shedding a tear for the fate of their ancestors, Quebecers are crying a little, unknowingly, for themselves."[96] The contemporary Québécois are oblivious as to how the past is structuring and shaping the present. As Dimitrios Karmis rightly notes, the hypothesis of false consciousness underlies Dufour's somewhat sorrowful, chagrined lines.[97]

Using concepts drawn from psychology to analyze the Québécois collectivity, Dufour asserts that this original hurt (the abandonment and Conquest) gave rise to an identity condition which may be likened to a "neurosis that makes an individual yearn intensely for several incompatible things at the same time."[98] This neurotic identity, he argues, has made the Québécois chronically unable to do either of two things: sever their ties with the former conqueror or give up the dream of independence for good. The result of this neurosis is the political ambiguity incessantly lambasted by the melancholy nationalist intellectuals. The solution is to exorcise the "demons that have been haunting Quebec for more than two centuries and that mortgage its future, whatever that future may be."[99] Yet Dufour stands apart from the other intellectuals studied here in that he does not envisage sovereignty as the cathartic break with the past which is absolutely necessary to overcome repressed trauma. For him, the necessity of sovereignty appears to reside instead in the historical inability of Quebec and Canada to come to mutual recognition and to build an equitable system of shared sovereignty. Dufour sees the political ambiguity of Quebec francophones as an after-effect of the original trauma of 1760 but not as a structural flaw that is keeping Quebec from coming into its own.

Jean Larose and Cultural Malaise

In a somewhat different register, the literary theorist Jean Larose has, for over a decade now, been leading a debate on the cultural poverty of Quebec society. His contribution is plurivocal, replete with tensions – characteristics that distinguish it from those of the writers examined up to now. Indeed, Larose can be read as a pallbearer for the search for lost authenticity so dear to the melancholy writers. To begin with, he opposes any attempt to reify or objectify the Québécois identity: "Québécois is the name of a movement, not that of a state or being ... and saying 'specifically Québécois' stops the movement, freezes it; binds it to its image in the mirror at a given instant."[100] In Larose, identity is a process, a polyphonic narrative project that is constantly being reworked; and this, in fact, will be my position in chapter 4. The problem with the concept of identity, Larose argues pertinently, is its reference to the identical, to sameness; but "there is no modern identity without movement, fragmentation, disparity."[101] Identity must be interpreted as an "eternal putting into play." This is why he criticizes – correctly, in my opinion – the Quebec nationalist discourse that attempts to circumscribe and potentially close the borders of Quebec authenticity. "The greatest pitfall for the 'Quebec' identity is to fall under the spell of its own reflection in the mirror of the identical."[102]

However, Larose's critique of one variety of nationalist discourse goes no further than to problematize the search for a lost authenticity, the idea of self-realization as "unification of the self, unity regained, reunion, *return of the self to itself.*"[103] He does not, though, challenge the unabashedly melancholy, depressive interpretation of the Québécois identity articulated by the nationalist intellectuals; on the contrary, he breathes new life into it. Thus Larose considers Quebec to be a "culturally alienated society" going through years of "quiet darkness" (*petite noirceur*).[104] What is lost in the transition from great to quiet darkness, he thinks, is an awareness of the dark. It is the lucidity, the stirrings of consciousness, that is tragically absent from this chiaroscuro called Quebec; this diffuse alienation has become practically imperceptible. The false consciousness of the Québécois is a pervasive theme in Larose's writing. In his view, various cultural traits of contemporary Quebec bear the impress of "our history as a colonized people" or our "age-old French-Canadian inferiority complex."[105]

Like all the authors interrogated to this point, Larose is convinced of the persistence of Quebec's great historical torpor. He too applies psychoanalytic terms to the identity condition of contemporary Quebec, positing that "our collective fatigue resembles the creeping, insidious, crippling fatigue of certain neurotics."[106] And he too suggests that political sovereignty is the road to cultural revitalization and regeneration. In order to take its rightful place in history, Quebec – whose identity is "not yet realized" – must take the path of independence.[107] It is because it is not sovereign "that the Québécois culture is not at present giving out onto the universal."[108] Independence is perceived as the pathway to maturity, to the universal, to "the sovereignty of ideas." In short, Larose's thought breaks with the Quebec nationalist discourse the better to nestle back into it. Despite his sincere determination to conceptualize identity as an evolving, dissensual discursive space, Larose does not explain how his melancholy narrative of a fatigued, neurotic, adolescent, culturally alienated Quebec gets around historical (as opposed to metaphysical) essentialism, the binding of the Québécois identity to a static, shopworn image of itself. If, as Larose believes, "the Québécois existence suffers from a dearth of symbols,"[109] one is tempted to ask whether this tragic narrative of the Québécois identity might have something to do with the problem.[110]

Jean Larose is not the only one to detect this cultural malaise. In an era in which the international success of certain Quebec artists, athletes, and entrepreneurs has led to naive triumphalism in some quarters, the discourse on the cultural "poverty" or "backwardness" of Quebec is still in the air. One may recall, for example, the furor provoked by Hélène Jutras's *Quebec Is Killing Me,* in which she threw down the gauntlet to the Quebec intelligentsia with her ill-considered musings on our cultural mediocrity. From regretful, resigned approval to injurious reproof, her letters elicited reactions of all sorts, not to mention raising the debate to a hitherto unseen level of intensity. Yet she was only reprising familiar themes without much subtlety – witness her statement that "Quebec is dying because, little by little, its people are becoming stupider."[111] Ashamed of a people preparing to shun its destiny for the second time in fifteen years, she expressed her desire to leave this "ghetto of expectation, [whose] walls ... are as high as human stupidity and narrow-mindedness can make them."[112] Quebec independence, which she too likened to political adulthood, had become a utopian horizon (because of the inferiority complex etched into the Québécois being), and so flight into exile became the only option open to her.

Calm has returned since then, and Jutras's letters have largely been forgotten; and still the discourse on the cultural mediocrity, the anchorless identity of the Québécois nation, ticks on with the regularity of a grandfather clock. In fact, Yvon Montoya and Pierre Thibeault, the editors of a recent collection of interviews on the state of contemporary Quebec culture, believe that Jutras's diagnosis remains valid today.[113] Starting from a fertile intuition that our collective unconscious is the source of a skewed image of ourselves, the authors rehabilitate this hypothesis in roundabout fashion by invoking the "self-censorship" that has allegedly become deeply ingrained in our "mental structures": "It would appear that Quebec has not gotten beyond its self-censorship reflex, the one that the makers of the Quiet Revolution boasted they had rid us of. The censorship inherent in the organization of our thoughts prevents *Quebec* from honing its analysis to an extent that would enable us, as a community, to challenge any power, whatever its source ... In our view, [the self-censorship reflex] did not totally disappear from our cultural and mental structures during the Quiet Revolution."[114]

Furthermore, although they express trenchant criticisms of one variety of nationalist discourse, the authors are not immune to monolithic, all-encompassing identity representations. "Quebec" and "*the* Quebec culture" are frequently invoked, only to be critiqued. "*The Quebec culture* is a closed, repetitive representation of reality cantoned inside an inoperative mental space, a wheel turning empty."[115] This irresistible craving for generality, to borrow Wittgenstein's phrase, is typical of several of the intellectuals interviewed. René-Daniel Dubois, for example, reiterates his conviction that the subjectivity of the Québécois intellectual, his or her way of apprehending reality, is profoundly "fascist": "[fascism] is introjected, it is assimilated, in the minds of both intellectuals and artists."[116] The people are victims of a subtle and imperceptible self-censorship reflex (intellectuals such as Dubois excepted; naturally, they succeed in breaking with alienation by rejecting the nationalist orthodoxy); and in this way, they are excluded from discussion and debate about their collective future. For Dubois, Quebec is devoid of a civil society and of public space.

Some of the other intellectuals questioned about the state of Quebec culture in Montoya and Thibeault's book reprise the themes addressed in this chapter in rather more conventional terms. For example, multidisciplinary artist Geneviève

Letarte revives the argument that Quebec's cultural energy is dampened by its confused, shapeless, ambiguous political identity. When Letarte looks at the Québécois, what she sees is "a people tired of dragging their heavy, bulky identity around like a ball and chain, like an old carcass."[117] She perceives Quebec's identity and political ambivalence as the source of its "stagnation" or "ossification." And taking essentialist mania to rarely attained extremes, the novelist and essayist Maxime-Olivier Moutier dwells on the pathological nature of the Québécois identity, asserting that obsession constitutes the substance of the Québécois being. "I think the Québécois is an obsessive. An obsessive is basically someone who thinks instead of acting ... The Québécois is someone who backs away, who is afraid; someone who doesn't dare go forward because there is always a risk when you go forward. All of our artists suffer from this propensity to do nothing, to never make any effort, whether verbal or physical, to exist."[118] Since the only possible therapy for the Québécois is an affirmation of political independence, Moutier too believes that exile will be the only valid response to another failed referendum.[119]

The forum in which it is most surprising to observe the resurgence of the melancholy discourse is undoubtedly the new journal *Argument*, which bills itself as a pluralistic "discussion forum" in which a "new sensibility," until now muffled by the traditional ideological rifts, can find expression. This sensibility is said to emerge out of "a different experience of what it means to belong to the modern culture in this place."[120] Of course, I am not suggesting that *Argument* represents a homogeneous body of thought. On the whole, the journal takes up the demanding, unwieldy – almost unmanageable – challenge of pluralism rather well. Yet it is striking to find, under the pen of young contributors (some of whom have defined themselves in sharp opposition to the preceding generation),[121] the same plaintive and melancholy sensibility that I have described at length in this chapter. To take but one example, in an issue in which *Argument* "lays bare the inability of the Québécois to judge France outside our own *identity psychodrama*,"[122] Daniel Tanguay's perspective on Quebec is very much in keeping with the intellectual trajectory I have described. He tells how the desire "to throw off the French-Canadian and Québécois condition, to leap out of 'minority group status' in a single bound," underlay his irrepressible desire to live the European French experience.[123] Yet the return from this exile, for someone who had consented to a genuine "inner transformation," took the form of malaise, discomfort, disorientation, disenchantment – an impossible communion with his homeland. Rather than viewing this way of being and (co)existing as an increasingly normal attribute of identity pluralism, Tanguay holds it accountable for the "neurotic Québécois identity." Since they are ontologically insecure, ashamed of themselves, the Québécois inevitably feel threatened by the symbols of Great French Culture. As a "degenerate, ersatz French-speaking culture," Québécois culture can only define itself in categorical opposition to the *authentic* French-language culture, that of France; whence the persistence of "that long-standing Québécois execration of all things intellectual," which Tanguay accepts as an undeniable fact.[124] In short, he concludes, "the distressing persistence of defensiveness, if not outright hostility, towards France shows that our society has not really overcome its *identity handicap*."[125] Although Tanguay's ideas must not be conflated with those of *Argument* as a whole, we can nonetheless conclude that certain sensibilities expressed in its pages are the direct descendants of the melancholy nationalists.

This review of more recent work allows us to conclude that soul-searching and melancholy are not exclusive to the nationalist intellectuals who built "modern" Quebec and grew old with it. The narrative has now been taken up by young writers experiencing the same "homesickness." Obviously, they do not simply parrot the discourse, for the new narrators of the Québécois identity have expressed it in their own style; still, they have not transmuted it or fundamentally altered its nature. Even someone like Robert Lepage, who has done much to transmit a hypermodern image of Quebec abroad, believes that "we are profoundly colonized."[126] Equally surprising in their ambivalence are Jean-François Lisée and Alain Dubuc, both determined (despite their differences) to put an end to what one describes as our culture of "failure," the other as our culture of "losers"; implying by these terms that they consider the Québécois ethos still hopelessly prey to this hereditary abjection.[127]

The emphasis today is on the ambient cultural mediocrity in which Quebec bathes – mediocrity that is itself fed by historical shame and self-contempt. For many, contemporary Quebec's problems remain rooted in our native alienation. The identity and political ambiguity of the Québécois are still considered to be a malignant growth that must be excised. In the prose of the new narrators, the Québécois condition is synonymous with neurosis, crisis, handicap, psychodrama. As with Vallières, the fate of the Québécois collectivity is still seen as a "slow death" or a state of "prolonged mediocrity." In chapters 2 and 4 I shall explore the preconditions for a change of focus, for emancipation from this morose, melancholy narrative that has dominated discussion of identity in Quebec for more than half a century.

2

Towards a New Representation of Ourselves: Guy Laforest and Jocelyn Létourneau

Enlightenment is man's emergence from his self-imposed immaturity. Immaturity is the inability to use one's understanding without guidance from another. This immaturity is self-imposed when its cause lies not in lack of understanding, but in lack of resolve and courage to use it without guidance from another.

Immanuel Kant

I do not know whether we will ever reach maturity.

Michel Foucault

It will be recalled that "emergence from self-imposed immaturity" was the answer given by Immanuel Kant to the question "What is enlightenment?" Mature and enlightened individuals and peoples, wrote the German philosopher, are those who are able to guide themselves by their own lights. In this definition one recognizes the ideal of autonomy, the cornerstone of the Kantian critical philosophy. Now, the resemblance between Québécois nationalism and German romanticism has often been noted and can hardly be doubted. The search for authenticity that drives Québécois nationalism, at least those variants studied in chapter 1, undeniably draws a large part of its inspiration from early nineteenth-century German romantic thought. Echoing Herder's critique of the abstract rationalism of the Enlightenment, the Québécois nationalist intellectuals proclaim (among other things) that human beings can only fulfill their potential and discover their true identity within the confines of a nation and by immersion in a language that is much more than a mere instrument of communication.[1] In fact, it would not be without interest to venture a comparative reading of Herder and several of the more important dramatists of the Québécois identity condition.

Still, the importance of the ideals of the French Enlightenment and the Aufklärung cannot go without mention. As I have tried to show, the melancholy nationalists of each generation have been in search of normality, which they see as being embodied in some kind of national maturity. Using Kant's language, the nationalist intellectuals discussed here are calling on Quebec to "emerge out of its self-imposed immaturity." Although they rarely maintain that Quebec, staggering under the weight of its unhappy history, is wholly responsible for the agony of its maturation, the nationalist intellectuals are typically inclined to assert that the Québécois people lack "resolution and courage."[2] In short, the quest for national normality is driven by the normative concepts of both autonomy and authenticity.[3]

One of the certainties on which the melancholy narrative rests, then, is clearly the abnormality of Quebec's identity condition and political status (past and present). The thorough repression of an overly painful past and the internalization of the infantilizing gaze of the Other are said to be the source of a perpetually juvenile, inhibited, fatigued Québécois identity, an identity with which its holders have not really come to terms. This propensity to view Québécois identity in terms of decay and abnormality characterizes even those intellectuals who have sought to break away from the nationalist narration of history as a litany of ills and abuses. For example, the political scientist Léon Dion, remarking on how "our literature is filled with whimpers, moments of despair about our past,"[4] offered the salutary corrective that "nations affirm and live their identity by representing their present and anticipating their future, not so much by reopening the wounds of their past."[5] Yet despite this determination to wrest the Québécois identity from the grip of the melancholy narrative, Dion's critique remains, in epistemological and narrative terms, a quasi-departure. He cannot manage to part with the image of an abnormal, watered down, adulterated, and ipso facto inauthentic contemporary Québécois identity. Dion writes: "Unfortunately, the identity that [the francophones] are seeking does not often bear the stamp of authenticity. It is but a copy of the foreign original ... The French Canadians, especially among the upcoming generation, experience modernity (or postmodernity) with the uncertainty of an insecurely anchored identity, an uncertainty just as sterile and even more pathetic than in the past."[6] It is clear to Dion that the contemporary Québécois identity (faithful in this to the old French-Canadian identity) fails the test of maturity, normality, and authenticity; he remained a melancholy intellectual. That said, his melancholy does not derive from a memory of historical trauma but, rather, from what I see as an erroneous interpretation of the present: that is, a misunderstanding of the plural, hybrid, labile nature of contemporary authenticities. As I shall attempt to show in chapter 4, the contours of both individual and collective authenticity must be redefined in light of the deep and pervasive diversity of contemporary societies.

Dion is not the only Quebec nationalist intellectual who, while seeking to break away from our national litany, remained convinced of the abnormality of our condition. Even Gérard Bouchard, who elucidates how the nations of the New World (the Americas, Australia) often draw upon "depressive myths" in discussing and giving meaning to their condition, feels that a *true*, mature, and authentic Québécois identity has not yet appeared. In the long run, he believes, such an identity can only grow out of a broad national coalition comprised of Quebec citizens from varied backgrounds and horizons rallying around a common language (French).[7] Bouchard, despite the originality of his research, remains inhabited by the Québécois melancholy I have been discussing. As Jocelyn Létourneau rightly notes, Bouchard in turn "takes up the eternal lament of unfulfilled destiny and the culture that has never found full expression."[8] According to Bouchard, "perfectly legitimate – indeed, fundamental – collective tendencies and aspirations are still awaiting expression ... There is a continental dream, an American dream, slumbering here, captive to our ambiguities and hesitations."[9] His innovative position, then, still conforms to the tradition of condemning the Québécois for their identity travails. My own intent, it should be said, is not to run the steamroller of normality over Quebec's specificity, as some revisionist historians have done; but I will attempt to show that it is no longer possible today to posit a causal relationship between the plural nature of identities, on the one hand, and their abnormality or the ontological insecurity of a people, on the other.

Nor is it a matter of impugning or mocking the sorrow meted out in the work of the melancholy writers, for it distills a widely shared way of living and feeling Quebec. There can be no doubting that Quebec was once an internal colony, a society essentially existing in a state of heteronomy. And moreover, whether the national alienation described by the nationalist intellectuals is or was real, imagined, or projected, it cannot be denied that it is in fact felt, *experienced*. This discourse simply cannot be consigned to the past with the peremptory claim that it is not representative. As Charles Taylor has taught us, it is on the basis of a particular narrative of identity that we can imagine alternative narratives.[10] The melancholy narrative, although less prevalent nowadays, will surely continue to pervade the interpretation of identity in Quebec for much time to come. However, one may well wonder what proportion of the Quebec population relates to this narrative and its gloomy overtones, as well as whether the fatigue described by Larose and others really does constitute the hard core of the Québécois identity. To what extent do the postulates of a weary, apathetic Quebec – with its collective unconscious draining all its creative and emancipatory energy, its political ambivalence tending towards suicide – answer to narrative dictates rather than phenomenological ones? It is impossible, in answering these questions, to tap directly into reality, to remove the filter of our own representations. But we do know that an increasing number of voices are speaking up to challenge this narrative enterprise and its unitary historical referent. New forms of *québécité* are being experienced within the (shifting) boundaries of Quebec authenticity.

This recasting of our identity does not necessarily imply a cutting of ties with memory and the past, but it may imply a different relationship to history. Above all, it demands the emergence of new narratives, new ways of talking about and representing ourselves, so as to accommodate sensibilities that cannot relate to the depressive myths created and maintained by the melancholy intellectuals. We are confronted with the task of elaborating new "persuasive fictions" that offer a somewhat better fit with the many ways of living and experiencing *québécité*.

Serge Cantin believes that today's attempts to theorize the Québécois identity as a collection of diffuse or fragmented representations basically reveal the depth of the theorists' own alienation.[11] Yet there are antecedents in Quebec thought for conceptualizing our identity in non-monist terms and, in particular, for doing so outside the Procrustean dichotomy of separatism as the necessary route to normality and maturity, on the one hand, and cosmopolitan anti-nationalism, on the other. One need not create a completely new discursivity to show how movement and *métissage* are integral to the Québécois identity. André Laurendeau (despite his occasional tendency to melancholy), Guy Laforest, and Jocelyn Létourneau are examples of those who have smudged the dividing lines between "inside" and "outside." To my mind, they have broken new ground with their dynamic interpretations of the Québécois identity, yet they have not succumbed to the sirens of anti-nationalism.

ANDRÉ LAURENDEAU: A FORERUNNER

One-time *Le Devoir* editor André Laurendeau has numerous spiritual heirs, yet his name is infrequently invoked in writings and discussion on the history of ideas in Quebec. Since the national question – in particular, the opposition between secessionist nationalism and anti-separatism – occupies a large part of that history, an œuvre as subtle and tension-filled as Laurendeau's tends to be passed over. And this tendency is accentuated by the low esteem in which the contributors to both *Parti pris* and *Cité libre* held his affirmationist nationalism. On the one hand, the nationalists, who have never wavered from their view of Quebec identity and political ambivalence as a chronic pathology, were bound to repudiate Laurendeau's cherished vision of a Canada both bilingual and bicultural. On the other, Trudeau and the partisans of a uninational Canada founded on the primacy of individual rights were more perturbed by Laurendeau's non-secessionist nationalism than by the liberation struggle of *Parti pris*. Indeed, as Guy Laforest puts it, "in the realm of ideas, [Laurendeau] much more than René Lévesque was Pierre Trudeau's real adversary."[12] Laurendeau's importance is that he was one of the first to reject the forced choice between secessionist nationalism and anti-nationalism.

Of Laurendeau's own nationalism, it cannot be said that it was monolithic. From an intellectual education as a protégé of Lionel Groulx to his co-chairing of the Royal Commission on Bilingualism and Biculturalism and his European sojourn, Laurendeau's thinking exhibited continuity and innovation in equal measures.[13] For the purposes of this discussion, I shall focus on his late writings. Though he never repudiated Groulx, the Laurendeau of the 1960s was well aware of the ever-growing interpenetration of cultures. And rather than condemn this hybridization, he sought to lay the ground work for a Quebec nationalism that could encompass both the "precarious being" of the Québécois people and the increasingly hybrid nature of its ethos.[14]

That is, the existence of a Quebec *nation* that had to be defended and promoted was unquestionably a fundamental premise of Laurendeau's thinking. His reflections on the nature of Quebec nationalism and Canadian federalism always took Quebec's needs as a starting point. But the Canadian federation of the 1960s did not offer Quebec the necessary political framework for its emancipation; in fact, to Laurendeau, the constitutional status quo looked intolerable.[15] One senses the urgency he felt when reading his General Introduction to the first volume of the *Report of the Royal Commission on Bilingualism and Biculturalism*. Where the future of Canada was concerned, Laurendeau wrote that the commission would lead "either to its break-up, or to a new set of conditions for its future existence."[16] He laid out the principles of a far-reaching and ambitious constitutional reform, in which francophones would be guaranteed access to services in their language and would "identify [themselves] with the political institutions and the symbols of [their] country."[17] More fundamentally, the equality of the founding peoples of Canada *as peoples* had to become, as he put it, the "mainspring" of the Canadian federal system. This system should not concern itself solely with individual equality before the law but also with the rights of communities: "it is not cultural growth and development at the individual level which is at stake, but the degree of *self-determination* which one society can exercise in relation to another."[18] Possessed of a remarkable intuitive sensibility, Laurendeau believed that the individual equality promoted by political liberalism "can fully exist only if each community has, throughout the country, the means to progress within its culture and to express that culture."[19] Yet for him, this cultural equality was nowhere in sight in the Canada of the late 1960s. French was not an official language. The francophone communities of Canada were vastly under-represented in official institutions and, more importantly, had little power to determine their own fate. Besides, the bicultural nature of Canada tended to be denied by the anglophone majority.[20]

In Laurendeau, then, there was nothing of the unconditional defender of Canadian federalism. Yet Quebec independence, a prospect he took seriously, was not the political option he preferred for his homeland.[21] The reason most often invoked by commentators attempting to justify Laurendeau's reluctance to support the Quebec separatist movement was his resistance to the hegemony of the United States. In Laurendeau's view, only by joining forces could Quebec and Canada stand firm against that south wind of homogenization.[22] But for Quebec and Canada to form a common front, the Canadian federation had to come in for a major reworking. To be specific, what Laurendeau had in mind was an asymmetrical federalism that would recognize Quebec as a "distinct society" and respect provincial prerogatives. But as history would have it, that dualist vision of Canada did not withstand the pan-Canadian nationalism formulated and advocated by Trudeau. As we shall see with Laforest, what was occluded by the victory of Trudeau's national vision was another very distinct version of the "Canadian dream."

GUY LAFOREST: GETTING OVER THE CONQUEST

Getting over the Conquest means hoping that, in Quebec, resentment will retreat into the interstices of society.

Guy Laforest

For more than ten years now, Université Laval political philosopher Guy Laforest has been striving to recast the foundations of Quebec nationalism. His focus remains on the vexed relationship between nationalism and political liberalism in the Canada/Quebec context.[23] With others, he has attempted to lay the groundwork for a liberal nationalism in which respect for individual rights does not entail the dismantlement of collective rights.[24] According to Laforest, an ever-precarious and unstable balance must be struck between nationalist demands and the primacy of individual rights.

Thus, for example, he believes that individual rights, so often violated in this century, must be enshrined in a charter of rights and freedoms. However, since individual freedom takes shape and substance within a shared tradition and belonging, national minorities must be recognized in the terms they use to represent themselves; in particular, they must possess the political autonomy necessary to safeguard and (re)produce their identity. Following from these basic considerations, Laforest conceives of Quebec as a pluralistic distinct society in which the defence and promotion of a national identity, comprising a common language and a range of institutions, is consonant with allowing citizens to view their own identity as plural and, as a result, to have a different feeling of allegiance to Quebec.[25]

This vision of Quebec as a pluralistic distinct society clashes with the Trudeauist symbolic universe, in which Canada is a uninational federation founded on legal equality between the provinces, just as it clashes with the melancholy narrative built around a tragic, unitary vision of history to which all must refer or else be accused of inauthenticity. As I mentioned in my introduction, Laforest is the author of one of the best-structured critiques of the Canadian federal configuration arising from the unilateral patriation of the Constitution. He sees the enactment of the Constitution Act of 1982 without Quebec's consent as the source of a new Canadian nationalism, the foundation of a pan-Canadian identity, and an alteration of the balance of power that collides frontally with Quebec's wish to conceive of itself as a nation, a distinct society, and an autonomous political community. The failure of the various attempts at constitutional renewal exemplifies the success of this enterprise of refounding the country. A (Canadian) nation has been erected, Laforest concludes, on the ashes of a federation; in 1982

"Canada was reconstructed with absolute and total contempt for the ideas that Laurendeau held dear: national duality, distinct society in Quebec, asymmetrical federalism."[26]

From his observation of this violation of the conventions of mutual recognition, reciprocity, coordination, and consent that must, he believes, be central to federated political entities, Laforest infers the moral illegitimacy of the current Canadian constitutional order. By this reasoning, the legitimacy of the sovereigntist project rests much more on a breach of trust and an abuse of power than on a set of historical grievances. Thus Laforest's nationalism bears no resemblance to the quest for normality, the desire for "reconquest" – recovery of our identity from the clutches of the past – that constitutes the cornerstone of the melancholy narrative. If he is trenchant on the subject of Canadian unitarist federalism, he is just as critical of the type of nationalism described in chapter 1.

Specifically, Laforest does not believe in the historical and theoretical necessity of Quebec independence. A nation, he thinks, can very well emancipate itself outside the confines of the nation-state model. Independence, or the construction of a nation-state, is not a prerequisite to reaching maturity, to transforming a collective consciousness occupied by the Other, or to an exorcism of a past that is killing the present. In other words, he does not consider Quebec sovereignty to be the cathartic break or the "psychological disengagement" (Vadeboncœur) essential to Quebec's emancipation. What Quebec needs is recognition of its identity, as well as a guarantee that the powers it must possess in order to defend its existence will not be curtailed or modified without its consent. Such a political status could take the form of sovereignty, but asymmetrical, multinational federalism would also serve the purpose. "In moral and political terms, I think both federalism and independence have claims to legitimacy in the history of Quebec," argues Laforest in this regard.[27] In no sense is the nation-state perceived as "the *normal* status of a *normal* people," in the stock language of separatist pedagogy. There is simply nothing abnormal or aberrant about federated peoples.

This critique of the discourse of normality and the historical necessity of independence does not find favour with those who sing the praises of decolonization. Even Pierre Vadeboncœur, one of the more interesting melancholy intellectuals, has never doubted the historical necessity of independence. "Looking ahead to 1987, I assume that independence will be a *fait accompli*, since it is reasonable and depends only on the continuation of a process that is well underway and likely to continue," wrote Vadeboncœur in 1977.[28] In other words, he views sovereignty as the normal, logical, and necessary outcome of Quebec's fitful, spasmodic striving towards autonomy. Supporting independence in Quebec, in Vadeboncœur's narrative, is tantamount to "standing up" and "making history instead of being made by it." Liberty, it seems, can only take the path of independence. In the interim, Quebec is only marking time, letting itself be taken in by the ruses of History. The Quebec of the melancholy nationalists is stuck in an endless vigil.

Laforest sees the orthodox tendency of Quebec nationalism as "the one that knows where reason and History are necessarily leading Quebec."[29] For his part, he takes issue with any eschatology or linear philosophy of History – whether that of a liberal such as Trudeau, for whom History "is tending toward the melting of nationalisms into larger federal wholes," or that of nationalists such as Vadeboncœur and Marcel Rioux, who believe that "national independence, and in particular Quebec independence, obey the logic of historical evolution."[30] Laforest considers these two teleological discourses to be of a piece. He maintains that "we are wrong when we lock up a people in a particular destiny."[31] In his renarration of the Québécois identity, he posits that the enlightened minds who would make Quebec sovereignty an obstacle on the path of Reason in History are off the mark; but "equally wrong are those who compare Quebec independence to a necessary transition from acne-ridden, tormented adolescence to the serene maturity of adulthood."[32] More Aristotelian, Laforest argues that the faces of prudence are manifold and highly likely to change over time. Maturity is a long struggle that may find expression in different political structures.

From a normative point of view, Laforest's critique of orthodox Québécois nationalism takes the form of a recommendation or, rather, a challenge: get over the Conquest. He thinks that the will to recover a lost dignity risks being tainted with historical resentment and revanchism. And indeed, these qualities characterize the most radical anti-colonialist positions considered in chapter 1. The melancholy intellectuals, as I have discussed at length, maintain that Quebec never recovered from the trauma of abandonment and the Conquest. Since then, with the gaze of the Other becoming layered over the self-image of Quebec francophones, alienation and "depersonalization" (Bouthillette) have come to stand in for subjectivity. Resentment is the consequence of continually staring at the "still-open wound"[33] of our past (a past associated with subordination to the British). Laforest, meanwhile, thinks that "overcoming resentment is the greatest challenge of our history."[34] At the dawn of the twenty-first century, only a kind of nationalism open to different ways of experiencing history can rally a profoundly pluralistic Quebec society. Getting over the Conquest does not mean giving up one's past but, rather, accepting the coexistence of memory processes that may be compatible or contradictory. It also means acknowledging that "ambivalence of being" is not a neurotic condition, and that political normality and modernity are no longer associated exclusively with independence. To quote Laforest:

Wishing Quebec to get over the Conquest is not the same as acting as if it never happened. On the contrary, it is hoping that we come to acknowledge it lucidly, without falling into the resentment associated with any enterprise of reconquest. Getting over the Conquest means accepting the identity of a plurinational distinct society for Quebec, and it also means recognizing that the institutions of British parliamentarianism belong as much to us as to anyone; finally, it means admitting that in a society in which French should be the common language, English is also one of our historical languages. In a word, it means accepting the hybridity of Quebec.[35]

Through the filter of their tragic vision of history and existence, the melancholy writers have fashioned an image of a vanquished, wounded, traumatized, unconscious homeland. In this narration of the Québécois identity condition, in which the Québécois tend to play the role of the victim, a univocal historical throughline provides the only point of reference. Yet in contemporary Quebec, this vision is far from drawing a consensus. Many Quebecers, including descendents of French Canadians, do not relate to it. What is more, this discourse is directed exclusively at the imagined French-Canadian community, and hence it is incompatible with the polyethnic and multinational nature of Quebec society. For these reasons, Laforest does not attempt to fix the Québécois identity condition within a reading of history or an agenda that is overdetermined by a founding trauma; instead, he tries to develop a political framework in which Quebecers can freely express the polyphony of their identities and their processes of memory.

JOCELYN LÉTOURNEAU AND "AMBIVALENCE OF BEING"

It is in the invention of a new relationship to culture, as memory and horizon, that the Québécois identity will eventually be redefined.

Jocelyn Létourneau

With Laforest, the dual identity of a significant majority of Quebecers ceases to be likened to a vice or a symptom of profound mental colonization. He has always urged sovereigntists to take seriously the "Canadian dream" of Quebecers who want to live in a multinational society characterized by asymmetrical federalism. He does not reduce this dream (cherished by Laurendeau, as we have seen) to the supposed ontological insecurity of the Québécois, but associates it with a desire to live in a political framework in which different peoples can coexist without having to renounce their primary collective identity. The sovereigntists, concludes Laforest, should not trivialize or deride this vision of the country in the name of a fictitious national maturity or normality. Their duty is rather "to put themselves in the shoes of their fellow citizens, who have the dismayed impression that their real country died when a certain idea of Canada disappeared."[36]

Of all our contemporary observers, it is perhaps Université Laval historian Jocelyn Létourneau who has done the most in recent years to depathologize the dual and overlapping allegiances of a large majority of Quebecers. Writing from a perspective that broadly coincides with that of this essay, Létourneau looks at what he calls the "founding pessimism" of certain Québécois intellectuals. In his view, the melancholy narration of the Québécois experience flows from these intellectuals' own discouragement and affliction, rather than from a genuine analysis of the historical evolution of French-speaking Quebecers. In other words, all the phenomena depicted by the melancholy narrators – cultural fatigue, chronic indolence, relegation to the margins of History, "tragic destiny," "desolation of lived experience" – are primarily a function of their own disenchantment; but, Létourneau maintains, they do not and have never corresponded to the historical experience of French-speaking Quebecers. These intellectuals have wilfully reconstituted a historical trajectory modelled on their tragic interpretation of the community's historical evolution. Noting the disparity between their own identity narrative and the ways in which francophone Quebecers feel and experience their identity, the melancholy intellectuals have never stopped "lecturing and reproving this group who refuse their predicted destiny, either by being unfaithful to the identity which they were assigned or by refusing to free themselves from their alleged subordination."[37] They cry out in unison (along with Vadeboncœur in the subtitle of his book, "To be or not to be") that "a people which does not assert itself will perish."

As a consequence of the superimposition of this discursivity on the lived experience of the Québécois, these writers categorically condemn identity ambivalence with a single voice. Serge Cantin writes: "It is a very grave mistake to think that we can survive much longer in a state of ambivalence,"[38] the spectres of extinction, assimilation, and soft genocide haunting his prose. As we have seen, the Québécois are being asked to draw upon their innermost resources to find the "courage of freedom," to give up the comfort of ambivalence.

Guy Laforest and Jocelyn Létourneau

What is at stake with this call for a cathartic break is the freedom of the Québécois people. But Létourneau thinks that certain melancholy intellectuals may be desiring this outcome on the basis of an erroneous conception of the "ambivalence of being" of the francophone Quebecers, and his project is to imagine a different hermeneutic scheme. The hermeneutic approach in philosophy is based on a dialectical relationship between the interpreter and the interpreted. The interpreted – that is, the identity condition and historical vicissitudes of the francophone Quebecers – is understood and evaluated in the light of the interpreter's concerns and values. In the melancholy hermeneutics, for example, the dual and overlapping historical belonging of a significant majority of Quebecers, their long history of non-separatist nationalism, is interpreted by those who condemn ambivalence and indolence, assert the historical and theoretical necessity of independence, and so on.

Proposing to break with this interpretive tradition, Létourneau suggests a new research hypothesis: "What if [French-speaking Quebecers] had found their freedom precisely in a non-space (*hors-lieu*) of identity called ambivalence of being, and what if this very thing constitutes an emancipated, consummated identity, rather than an alienated or constrained one?"[39] Instead of being a "problem to solve," the francophones' identity ambivalence becomes, for Létourneau, a phenomenon to be studied, a fact to be reckoned with. Indeed, he assigns an ontological status to it: "the locus of being of the Québécois, the place they inhabit, is ambivalence; ... this ambivalence is the only permanent feature of their condition, the only invariant providing continuity over time."[40] Létourneau's ontology, like Dumont's (though the two are antinomic), is profoundly historicized, temporal. By sifting through the accretions, the accumulations of things, events, and ideas left by history, both unearth the identity condition of Quebec francophones. In Létourneau's case, ambivalence is not perceived as an essence, encoded in the Québécois' genes or written in their soul, but as the product of a historical process in which they have sought to mediate, often laboriously, between a primary identification with Quebec and a profound attachment to Canada.

Létourneau adds a moral and political judgment to this reading of history; that is to say, this dual affiliation does not stem from the consubstantial cowardliness of the Québécois being, nor is it a suicidal political stand. Wearing one's identity ambivalence proudly "is no betrayal of the ancestors, or an expression of alienating hesitation or pitiable 'false self-consciousness,' but a reclaiming, a reintegration, of the reflexive wisdom of the ancestors into the construction of a present and a future defined along the lines of a calculated risk; that is, sensitive reason."[41] For Létourneau, identity and political ambivalence are functions of prudence and wisdom. Validated by practical reason, ambivalence ceases to be synonymous with decline, decrepitude, or unconsciousness. Likewise, Létourneau refuses to compare the Québécois identity to a type of childhood or immaturity. The metaphor of the child derives from a "diagnostic error" and must be deconstructed: "Quebec is not unfinished; it does not resemble a child who is slow in entering adulthood and who rejects the concomitant responsibilities."[42]

Reasoning thus, Létourneau is led to reject the argument that Quebec emancipation depends on a refoundation of its identity and political framework. Aquin, Dumont, and Cantin, as we have seen, have asserted the necessity of refounding the country – not by denying the past, as Jean Lesage's Quiet Revolutionaries did,[43] but by acknowledging and coming to terms with the traumas and burdens of our history. This refoundation, as a clear manifestation of a collective will to emerge from the margins of history, would mark the end of avoidance, flight, repression, and denial. Even some intellectuals of the new generation, albeit well aware of how present the traumas of the past were to some of their predecessors, seem convinced of the need to place Quebec on a new symbolic and political footing. For example, Marc Chevrier contends that the absence of debate around the idea of republicanism in Quebec and the "interminable" discussion on the nature of the Québécois nation are partly a function of the ineffectual, ambiguous foundations of our political system. In his words, the problem of defining the nature of the Quebec nation

> is linked in part to the foundations of our political regime. Quebec has never experienced a founding political event, a solemn act in which the people participate in choosing the community's ideals, principles and institutions. Still without their own written constitution, and perhaps as a result of having missed this very formative experience of citizenship, Quebecers grope their way through history ... All Quebecers – by birth and by adoption – should have access to the tremendous pleasure of being able to govern themselves. They should be able to define the political framework of their coexistence and their participation in a common citizenship. For this to happen, they will need to establish a new regime.[44]

In this account, a Québécois people of modest political origins is condemned to fumble endlessly through history. Only the device of a flamboyant political renaissance (embodied in the republican ideal), to which all citizens can relate, would bring Quebec out of its long-standing idleness and attune it to the great ideals of liberty and political participation.

But the philosopher James Tully, in his remarkable genealogy of modern constitutionalism, puts us on guard against the reification and glorification of political origins. A univocal reference to a founding moment can hinder intercultural accommodation, homogenize competing or minority interpretations of the past and projections into the future, and in so doing, contribute to the marginalization of difference. The fetishization of foundations seems ill-suited to social fabrics marked by heterogeneity. This is why Tully suggests that a constitution be considered, not as an inviolable contract ratified in a distant past, but as a set of non-definitive agreements arising from intercultural dialogues occurring at different points in time.[45] In other words, a political association is profitably seen as developing within a flexible framework that is open to deliberation and amendment, letting citizens and groups debate the recognition of their identities, the distribution of resources, the sharing of power, and so on. In this view, citizens' dignity and freedom depends more on an opportunity to change the rules of the game of political association as their identities change than on making a myth out of a founding political act. Moreover, even if Chevrier is right to assert that France in no way epitomizes republicanism or exhausts its possibilities, and that republicanism should not be reduced to Jacobinism, it remains to be demonstrated that a republic could be built in Quebec out of the pluralism of our society. Although the tradition of civic humanism to which he adheres has a number of merits, it must be admitted that it has difficulty coming to grips with the deep diversity of contemporary societies.[46] Chevrier cannot be faulted for giving consideration to the conditions of fuller political participation in Quebec, but one can legitimately doubt the capacity of his republican ideal to meet the challenges facing a multicultural, multinational society in a time of modernity profoundly marked by movement, fragmentation, and various forces of disintegration. There are no grounds for asserting at this time that citizens who define their identities in many different ways could rally around a founding political event. Chevrier's project depends on a unitary political subject who is exceedingly hard to find in the socio-cultural landscape of contemporary Quebec.[47]

Even the philosopher Daniel Jacques, though more sensitive to the pluralistic, fragmented nature of the Québécois identity, seems to subscribe to this fetishization of foundations. He writes, "If Canada and Quebec remain societies marred by confused allegiances, it is because their respective destinies are unfolding without having been properly founded."[48] Jacques believes that it is on the basis of a "solid foundation" – that is to say, "an event that has meaning and legitimacy in the eyes of all citizens and that constitutes a moment of beginning, the start of a new history" – that the various national communities of Quebec can transcend resentment to form a genuine political community.[49] This may be a noble endeavour, but it is hard to see how citizens upholding different identities, values, and interests can manage to reach definitive agreement on the terms of such a solemn pact. Once again, it seems more realistic to argue, with Tully, that "the form of culturally diverse democracy that will be both free and stable in the twenty-first century is one in which the prevailing rules of recognition are always open to challenge and modification by the diverse members."[50] I shall explore this position further in chapter 4.

This digression enables me to point up the originality of Létourneau's political thought in the Quebec intellectual context. What he is offering is a conception of politics and democracy that may be termed "agonistic." Unlike the majority of the thinkers I have discussed, Létourneau does not seek the conditions for national reconciliation or societal consensus; he wants to build a conception of politics that takes account of the irreducible tensions (not necessarily antagonisms) between the different Quebec communities.[51] Like Tully, he sees identity and recognition politics as no different from other forms of politics; that is, as an ongoing activity aimed at alleviating conflict and striking ever-precarious compromises.[52] The national communities of Quebec, he argues, have no need to converge towards a founding act that will result in unanimity; what they need is a public space where different authenticities can meet, interact, agree on certain directions for society, express their disagreement, critique one another's positions, and so forth. The telos of this agonistic activity is not definitive agreement on the terms of political association and the conditions of mutual recognition; it is the creation of a deliberative space enabling groups and citizens to disclose their identity and political demands, and correlatively, to have themselves heard by the other members of society. The political community is understood here as an open-ended process, entertaining a dynamic relationship with its origins (rather than staggering under the weight of history), and already very much a part of "normality." Létourneau thinks of Quebec

> as a community in constant evolution, in permanent tension with the society and the socialities on which it is built, which it inspires and negates at the same time. A community that is neither consummated nor unconsummated. A community with an untheorizable, unforeseeable trajectory. A community whose borders are continuously crossed by its "subjects." A community determined by history instead of one that determines it. A community existing as an open-ended process, rather than constantly relating back to an original seed planted by the ancestors and demanding a future of continuity.[53]

Létourneau contradicts those who would force Quebec to fit into a philosophy of history, as well as those who believe in its necessary refoundation. He does not inveigh against the ambivalence of being of the Québécois; he takes it as a given and attempts to adumbrate a concept of democracy rooted in the complexity of our identity.

Although Laforest and Létourneau clearly share Laurendeau's heritage, their narrative breaks with that of the principal melancholy authors. They are sketching out and advocating a new representation of ourselves, enabling us to extricate ourselves from the tragic version of the Québécois identity narrative. Like Foucault, Laforest and Létourneau see the conquest of maturity as an unending task, one that is not and can never be fully realized. In this respect, the Quebecers are no different – that is, no less mature – than other peoples. What is more, Létourneau and Laforest do not consider the dual belonging or ambivalence of being shared by a fair majority of Quebecers as some sort of hereditary defect. But make no mistake, this contention is akin to a heresy among Quebec nationalists. Even Gérard Bouchard, in his book on the Quebec nation, chose to ignore the fact that a large majority of Quebecers identify strongly with Canada; he perceives this dual identification as a characteristic of which we must rid ourselves through the expedient of a Quebec nation, which would then become our only locus of identity. In addition to asking francophones to sacrifice one of their communities of belonging, the solution proposed by Bouchard can hardly meet the legitimate expectations of Quebec anglophones or the First Nations. He cordially invites the latter to take part in building the Quebec society of tomorrow and in rewriting its historical memory, but he implies that they must resign themselves to giving up their primary national identification. In rejecting the "plurinational" conception,[54] Bouchard offers Quebec's national minorities an a priori unacceptable pact. And yet there is a way of envisaging an inclusive Quebec, in which it is possible for an individual to belong to more than one nation, in which the political sphere does not try to rank citizens within a hierarchy or suppress their identity affiliations; a Quebec nation which therefore does not treat its national minorities the way it has been treated by the Canadian federation since 1982. Along with Dimitrios Karmis, I believe it is possible to imagine a Quebec nation that would be neither the sum of different ethnic enclaves nor the sole object of national identification for all its members.[55]

For the purposes of this study, the originality and importance of Laforest's and Létourneau's ideas reside in the fact that, though they forcefully critique the discourse of national normality and maturity, this does not lead them to embrace anti-nationalism; both theorists consider the nation to be a fundamental identity referent.[56] Naturally, their visions of Quebec diverge on several points. Laforest believes that the sovereigntist option no longer derives its legitimacy and vitality from the need to overcome collective alienation, but from the instating of a policy of unitarist federalism coupled with systematic non-recognition of Quebec's distinctness. The Canadian dream of the Québécois having turned into a nightmare, he believes that, once they have exhausted all their "ordinary" political and legal avenues, they may have to fall back on an open, pluralistic sovereignty-partnership arrangement.[57] Létourneau, for his part, takes the longer view of the Canada-Quebec constitutional impasse, opining that with less dogmatism and more "accommodating reason," the Quebec vision of Canadianness still has a chance of coming across. It is a matter, he says, of allowing new generations to succeed where the previous ones have failed. These differences are immaterial to my tentative sketch of an alternative interpretive tradition. The important issue has been to show that it is possible to interpret identity in Quebec outside the melancholy nationalist/anti-nationalist dichotomy and, in so doing, to look to a genuine tradition of thought – a minority tradition, it is true, yet one that is still alive and well in Quebec. This is the task I shall take up in chapter 4. Before that, however, we must explore the other pole of this enduring debate: the anti-nationalist discourse.

3

Identity within the Limits of Reason Alone: Anti-nationalism and Political Universalism

To this point in our exploratory mapping of the interpretations of identity in Quebec, we have examined a discourse in which the Québécois are stigmatized by their past, idling on the margins of History, grasping interminably after normality and maturity; a depressive Quebec, with the occasional stirrings of consciousness, but otherwise comfortably numb; a would-be nation in a state of constant vigil. This psychodramatic historical narrative has long served as a reference point for a broad range of intellectuals, artists, politicians, and others wishing to render the Québécois experience a little more intelligible and meaningful. But as they engage in this effort, these Quebecers are effectively writing and producing a national identity. As I mentioned in my introduction, an identity exists and persists by virtue of its being narrated; there is no reality that is not interpreted. In agreement with the hermeneutic tradition, it must be stated that identities are not objective, empirical data that can be collected with the neutral, sterile instruments of science but, rather, interpretations of lived experience, temporalized and structured into narratives that bind and order the past, present, and future of a community.[1]

However, to the intellectuals who contend that such identities are created from whole cloth by (nationalist) elites and passively taken on by apathetic, easily manipulable people, one may respond that the bearers of these identities also have the capacity for resistance, transgression, and transvaluation.[2] To suggest that identities are imposed from outside is to implicitly cast the intellectual in the role of a sounder of reveille for minds in thrall to the perfidy of nationalism. But in fact, the melancholy nationalist version of the Québécois identity has never been in a monopoly position. As we saw in the last chapter, Laurendeau, Laforest, and Létourneau have critiqued nationalist orthodoxy and contributed to the development of a language that can account for the dual belonging experienced by many Quebecers. They have countered one narrative, and its pretensions to hegemony, with an alternative one. Furthermore, between the defensive nationalism of Groulx and the separatism of *Parti pris*, the anti-nationalist liberal individualism of the early *Cité libre* found favour with many French Canadians. And despite its far-reaching intellectual influence, the Montreal school's reading of Quebec history was far from unanimous. As the historian Ronald Rudin reminds us, the Université Laval historians who were contemporaries of Frégault, Brunet, and Séguin preferred a quite different interpretation of Quebec's past, rejecting the cataclysmic reading of the Conquest and the British regime.[3]

In present-day Quebec, well-known and prolific intellectuals such as René-Daniel Dubois, Marc Angenot, Jean-Pierre Derriennic, Nadia Khouri, and Régine Robin continue to mount pointed opposition to nationalist discourse and politics.[4] Given this state of affairs, it is perplexing to find Angenot and Khouri claiming that a permanent state of censorship holds sway in Quebec. They write, "If there's one expression that can be transposed and suits Quebec, it's that of 'Single Orthodoxy' [*pensée unique*] ... Single Orthodoxy: omnipresence of the obsessional nationalism which serves as a touchstone, 'Quebec-centrism' or the wearing of blinkers to shut out the vast world, a childish Manicheism pitting 'us' against 'them,' or 'English Canada against Quebec.'"[5] It is not enough for these writers that the anti-nationalist standpoint has been a constant in the history of Quebec ideas since the mid-twentieth century; somehow it is still the exception that proves the rule of the single orthodoxy. Whereas Gérard Pelletier declared that "unanimity is dead" some forty years ago (in an essay on the decline of Catholic faith in Quebec), today's anti-nationalists decry the fact that it is still alive and well in politics. Only a handful of intellectuals, they claim, have remained true to their calling, sufficiently lucid to resist the spread of nationalist ideas; and none but the most enlightened of them are immunized against this contagion.

If so, then the totalitarianism reigning in Quebec must be so soft that it is possible for intellectuals to express their dissent in a myriad of contexts and forums.[6] Indeed, I hope that this chapter will serve to demonstrate the vitality of the critique of nationalism in Quebec. The nationalist intellectuals have always had to contend with rigorous, coherent opponents. Now it is legitimate to hope that a genuine dialogue will develop between the more serious proponents of both positions (each of which comprises several variants). Too often the most radical, least subtle commentators are the ones who square off in public. The telos of such encounters is certainly not a Foucaultian reciprocal elucidation; it is to delegitimate an adversary, to expel him or her from the democratic arena. The parties engage in polemics instead of putting themselves into play. When one turns a deaf ear, the other has no choice but to raise her or his voice.[7] One can only hope that the new Quebec intellectuals will adopt a different attitude and embark on the path to a genuine ethic of dialogue.

TRUDEAU AND THE CRITIQUE OF NATIONALIST (UN)REASON

The role of the journal *Cité libre* in the recent history of Quebec is well known. It was one of the rare forums in which intellectuals with varying perspectives and backgrounds mobilized to combat a common evil: the authoritarianism and clerical conservatism of the "Duplessis era." Perhaps a comment on the use of this term is in order; it is no doubt true that the division of our history into eras – the "Great Darkness" (Duplessis era), the "Quiet Revolution" – serves the needs of identity and narrative as much as and perhaps more than it corresponds to a series of radical transformations of our historical condition. The Great Darkness of Duplessism did not give way to enlightened modernity in the short period in which the Sauvé government held power. Throughout the twentieth century, slowly accumulating political, economic, and cultural changes paved the way for the accelerated modernization of the 1960s.[8] Notwithstanding this salutary caution expressed by certain of our historians, sociologists, and political scientists, it remains that the constellation of intellectuals who rallied around *Cité libre* felt the timidity, conservatism, traditionalism, and clericalism of French-Canadian society as an oppressive weight. If thinkers as different as Gérard Pelletier, Pierre Trudeau, Fernand Dumont, Marcel Rioux, Jean-Marc Léger, Gilles Marcotte, Charles Taylor, Adèle Lauzon, René Lévesque, Pierre Vadeboncœur, Pierre Vallières, and so many others made common cause in the pages of *Cité libre*, it was to combat this ossification of the

French-Canadian identity into retrograde categories, to reject the conflation of the political and the spiritual, and to fight systematic political corruption and the exploitation of the francophone proletariat. What each of them offered Quebec society were new ways of looking at itself – something it greatly and undeniably needed.

Now, the writings of these authors no more form a monolithic bloc than do those of the nationalists discussed in the preceding chapters. *Cité libre* brought together, "not minds, but people," with opposing views in many areas.[9] Overlying the elements of unity to be found in their writings is a multiplicity of views and concerns. Therefore I have chosen to focus on certain writings of Pierre Elliott Trudeau. Even Gérard Pelletier, who was most closely aligned with Trudeau overall, was not of one mind with him on all points. For example, in a look back at the beginnings of *Cité libre*, Pelletier stated that despite its opposition to "cultural nationalism," the journal never advocated "liberal individualism."[10] But liberal individualism was exactly the theoretical prism through which Trudeau came to view reality. When André-J. Bélanger states that "after a process of progressive decompartmentalization, the journal rather swiftly arrived at the universal man," and that "in so doing, it deprived him of belonging to a community, leaving him alone to face himself, or an image of the ideal man," he is referring primarily to the contributions of Trudeau, the dominant figure of the first *Cité libre* generation.[11] But clearly, the "liberal rationalism" or "atomism" that Bélanger rightly detects in the pages of *Cité libre* rather poorly characterizes the ideas of other contributors such as Dumont or Taylor.

For someone who formed an image of Trudeau at the end of his political career, in particular from his crusade against the Meech Lake accord, his youthful writings are striking –

indeed, astonishing. The gulf between the intellectual and the politician seems immense. To this it might be replied that it is "perfectly normal" for the intellectual to take a critical distance from current events, whereas the politician moves within the sphere of *doxa*, opinion, publicity, the ephemeral. There is an element of truth to this distinction; however, it does suggest an idealized and potentially outdated conception of the role and position of the intellectual. Be that as it may, with Trudeau, convictions verging on dogmatism appear to have been built on the ashes of a theoretical background rich in subtlety and nuance.

Along with historians such as Marcel Trudel, Jean Hamelin, and Fernand Ouellet, Trudeau was one of the fiercest opponents of the Montreal school in the 1950s. He never subscribed to the view that responsibility for the historical decline of the French Canadians rested with the English Canadians. He always found that "it was ridiculous for nationalists to claim that just about all of our backwardness was 'the fault of "les Anglais."'"[12] But Trudeau would not deny the difficulty of gaining acceptance and accommodation for the francophone fact in Canada. In addition to fighting unflinchingly against Canadian unilingualism, the young Trudeau waxed indignant at the absolutist leanings of the federal government. Ottawa, he argued, could not ignore and encroach upon provincial areas of jurisdiction with impunity.[13] He even argued that Anglo Canadian nationalism, "condescending" in more than one respect, had "produced, inevitably, French Canadian nationalism."[14] Imbued with the tradition of Montesquieu, Locke, and Tocqueville, Trudeau had made the principle of the balance of powers, weight and counterweight, the governing idea of his political thought. Consequently, he was compelled to defend provincial autonomy when he observed how the federal government's centralizing impulse lessened the provinces' capacity for resistance and opposition. In *Federalism and the French Canadians*, which remains his most important work, Trudeau went as far as to promote a kind of *cooperative* federalism in which relations between the levels of government would be characterized by dialogue and mutual respect for each one's prerogatives.[15]

Trudeau's purpose, in enunciating this critique of Canadian quasi-federalism, was to provide a corrective; obviously it did not make him into a French-Canadian nationalist. It is probably no exaggeration to state that Trudeau the intellectual abhorred all nationalisms in general and French-Canadian nationalism in particular. As I have written, he was especially exercised by the tendency of French-Canadian neo-nationalists to deny responsibility for their society's "backwardness" and deficiencies. For example, he refused to view the Conquest as a trauma sufficiently powerful to deaden the will and consciousness of Quebec francophones. The annexation of the French Canadians to the British Empire in 1763 was a historical fact; but still, he felt, the francophones possessed the means – even under the division of powers defined by the British North America Act – to take up the challenges of political modernity: "Whether or not the Conquest was the cause of all our woes, whether or not 'les Anglais' were the most perfidious occupying power in the history of mankind, it was still true that the French-Canadian community held in its hands *hic et nunc* [as of the early 1950s] the essential instruments of its regeneration: by means of the Canadian Constitution, the Quebec State could exercise far-reaching power over the soul of French Canadians and over the territory which they occupied – the richest and largest of all Canadian provinces."[16]

Anti-nationalism and Political Universalism

As Trudeau saw it, the task of *Cité libre* was not to deny the humiliations experienced by the French Canadians but to engage in consciousness-raising and empowerment. It was more important for the *Cité libre* writers to take part in the modernization of the state, democracy, and economy of Quebec than for them to add verses to a melancholy refrain they already found interminable. In the same vein, the French Canadians ought to learn to make optimal use of the powers and resources already granted to them before quarrelling with Ottawa to obtain new ones. In sum, French-Canadian neo-nationalism was feeding off the energy needed for the modernization of Quebec. Transvaluing received ideas, Trudeau maintained that although, allegedly emancipatory, nationalism was in fact "like a form of alienation ... it misdirected into struggles against 'les Autres' the very forces that were needed a thousand times over to stand up to the people ultimately responsible for our own utter poverty: our so-called élites."[17]

Trudeau's criticism was not limited to the French-Canadian and Quebec context: he considered nationalism, as a relationship to self and others, to be a theoretical aberration. Steeped in the heritage of the Enlightenment, Trudeau believed that reason, not the nation, is the true home of humanity. At first glimpse, the nationalism that Trudeau likens to shackles on the advance of Reason in History is not "a mere feeling of belonging to the nation" but a belief in the necessary fusion of state and nation.[18] He did not believe that political normality and maturity are necessarily embodied in a nation-state. For example, he rightly considered federalism to represent a better fit with pluralistic societies than the nation-state model. There is no need to quibble with Trudeau on this point; though they do not signify the end of sovereignty as such, the numerous federalizing processes marking our advanced modernity show that the era has passed when the international order was dominated and structured by nation-states.

Yet Trudeau's semantics lead him at times to blur certain important distinctions. In particular, where he begins by critiquing the normality and universality of the nation-state, he often shifts to a frontal attack on nation and nationalism understood as a feeling of belonging to or identifying with a nation. His notorious early 1960s diatribe against the Quebec nationalist intelligentsia, "New Treason of the Intellectuals," provides a good example of this characteristic blurring of distinctions. Just after an epigraph revealing Julien Benda's direct lineage with eighteenth-century thought, Trudeau opines, "It is not the concept of *nation* that is retrograde; it is the idea that the nation must necessarily be sovereign."[19] But further along, through a subtle semantic shift, his criticism of the nation-state turns to distaste for the very idea of a nation: "A concept of nation that pays so little honour to science and culture obviously can find no room above itself in its scale of values for truth, liberty, and life itself. It is a concept that corrupts all."[20]

Other writings of the former prime minister confirm his profound dissatisfaction with the concepts of nation and nationalism. He was a true son of the Enlightenment, driven by the ideals of individual liberty, autonomy, justice, and equality (understood as universal values that are always identical to themselves). In the image of certain anglophone liberal philosophers of the second half of the twentieth century, he remained impervious to critiques of the strongly universalistic Enlightenment concept of Reason. In Trudeau's eyes, the great unfolding of Reason in History on a grand scale was effectively being waylaid by nationalism. Nowhere is this equation of nationalism and unreason more patent than in his essay fittingly titled "Federalism, Nationalism and Reason." There was no doubt in Trudeau's mind that when the peoples of the earth are sufficiently mature and enlightened, nationalism as a world view will crumble and pile up with the already voluminous trash of history: "And just like clannishness, tribalism, and even feudalism, nationalism will probably fade away by itself at whatever time in history the nation has outworn its utility: that is to say, when the particular values protected by the idea of nation are no longer counted as important, or when those values no longer need to be embodied in a nation to survive."[21] Similarly, Trudeau had great hopes that "in advanced societies, the glue of nationalism will become as obsolete as the divine right of kings."[22] Thus in his philosophy of history, nationalism falters and collapses while reason progresses, is revealed, and is actualized. While federalism rests on a rational foundation, nationalism draws its attraction from the immaturity, insecurity, and emotionality of individuals. Therefore the task of the enlightened intellectual is to demystify the role of the nation and nationalism in fashioning personal identity. As we shall see with Angenot and Derriennic, the anti-nationalist intellectuals have repeatedly taken up this work of demystification.

Thus Trudeau places cold reason in opposition to the mystifying power of nationalism. This "rise of reason in politics" for him constitutes, "an advance of law"; he asks, "Is not law an attempt to regulate the conduct of men in society rationally rather than emotionally?"[23] Educated as he was in the classical tradition of political liberalism, Trudeau was referring here only to individual rights. As rational beings, all that individuals need is a "negative" conception of liberty, or the assurance that their rights and freedoms will not be arbitrarily violated, in order to emancipate and actualize themselves as human agents.[24] In any case, argued Trudeau, only the weak have any need to enjoy collective rights. This explained his opposition to granting any particular status to Quebec within the Canadian federation, an opposition he upheld and affirmed his whole life long. On the one hand, he believed that there is a basic contradiction between defining a particular status for Quebec and instating a universal, undifferentiated citizenship. On the other, he claimed that the demand for special status or collective rights for Quebec betrayed the survival of the old French-Canadian inferiority complex. Trudeau refused to insult the Québécois "by maintaining that their province needs preferential treatment in order to prosper within Confederation."[25] Quebec does not need "crutches" in order to confront the many tribulations of political and economic modernity.[26] I shall return in this chapter to what I see here as a wrong interpretation of the role of collective rights in the context of minority nations.

In addition to feeding the chronic cowardliness of the Québécois, collective rights, Trudeau argued, can only be instated at the cost of suppressing the individual rights of minorities and dissidents. In fact, he considered collective rights to be ethnocentric by definition. Since their purpose is to preserve and promote specific linguistic and cultural traits, collective rights impede the establishment of a purely civic nation in which the state only entertains ties with citizens in isolation. This view led Trudeau to state that "the nationalists – even those of the left – are politically reactionary because, in attaching such importance to the idea of nation, they are surely led to a definition of the common good as a function of an ethnic group, rather than of all the people, regardless of characteristics."[27] The assignment of collective rights – a necessary correlate of any nationalist policy – is, in Trudeau's view, an ethnic practice irreconcilable with the principles of equality, individual liberty, and undifferentiated citizenship on which liberal societies are founded.

Having examined Trudeau's critique of nationalism, coupled with his apology for liberal individualism, we can now sketch the outlines of his conception of identity and politics. Identification with a nation and loyalty to a culture are transitory stages in the development of individuals and peoples, which ultimately lead to an individualistic and universalistic political identity. Faithful to the spirit of the Enlightenment, Trudeau punctuates his discourse with allusions to this purposive advance of History. Thus the obscure ideological period in which nationalism reigns is a "transitional period in world history," one that is "crippl[ing] the advance of civilization."[28] Trudeau dreamed of the day when human beings would no longer need national and cultural reference points to give their lives meaning. He pinned his hopes for the future "on the fully developed man of intellect."[29] In short, Trudeau conceived of identity within the limits of reason alone. Of course, this conception of identity rests on the postulate of a univocal Reason, as well as the certitude that it must be embodied politically in universalism and cosmopolitanism. This is why Bélanger states that, with the *Cité libre* contributors and above all Trudeau, "the essential characteristic is openness to the world, that is, the abolition of cultural borders in favour of 'political, social, and economic universalism.'"[30]

It is surely not too bold to conjecture that we have here the ontological underpinnings of Trudeau's subsequent political action. He sought to make Canada into a civic, bilingual, multicultural, uninational political community founded on a shared allegiance to values such as absolute legal equality, symmetry among the provinces, tolerance for religious and cultural differences expressed (only) in the private sphere, and the inalienability of individual rights (except in times of crisis). The inhabitants of Chicoutimi, Kahnawake, or Victoria, being no different in kind, should enjoy the same rights and ultimately should present themselves as Canadians first and foremost. Put another way, Trudeau theorized a type of constitutional patriotism before the concept even existed. And so, guided by "cool-headed reason," he went so far as to propose the outright assimilation of the First Nations in his White Paper of 1969. He argued for the extinction of the treaties signed by the aboriginal peoples and the European colonizers: "I don't think that we should encourage the Indians to feel that their treaties should last forever within Canada so that they'll be able to receive their twine and their gunpowder. *They should eventually become Canadians as all other Canadians* ... and this is the only basis on which everyone in our society can develop as equals."[31] Trudeau, then minister of justice, had no choice but to relent when confronted with the indignation of the Native peoples, whose cultural renaissance was just getting underway.

But this rebuff in no way changed his conviction that transcending cultural boundaries was a prerequisite to progress. In this sense, the 1982 patriation of the Constitution and the instatement of the Canadian Charter of Rights and Freedoms were the consummation of Trudeau's political thought and career. Where before 1982 it was still possible to view the Canadian federation as a multinational entity resting on a contract between the founding peoples of Canada, this conception collapsed with the unilateral action of the federal government and the other provinces (thereby denying Quebecers their right to self-determination),[32] and with the enactment of a charter that renders provincial laws subject to being overruled at any time. Trudeau himself states it clearly: "the Canadian Charter was a *new beginning* for the Canadian nation: it sought to strengthen the country's unity by basing the sovereignty of the Canadian people on a set of values common to all, and in particular on the notion of equality among all Canadians."[33] In this way, he confirmed Dumont's analysis to the effect that the events of 1982 represented in some sense a "second founding" of Canada.

ANTI-NATIONALISM AND THE CRITIQUE OF ETHNICISM

Trudeau's heirs are numerous in Quebec and Canada. Academics, jurists, and politicians openly avow their heritage, and indeed a newly revived *Cité libre* was published at regular intervals in the 1990s. However, it would be wrong to assert that the new *Cité libre* carried the same genetic baggage as the old, just because people such as Pelletier and Trudeau once wrote for it. The journal of the 1950s and 1960s was a pluralistic, heterogeneous forum for discussion and debate in which intellectuals from vastly different backgrounds and horizons responded to one another, whereas the new *Cité libre* openly clamoured for "liberalism and Canadian unity." Writers such as Max Nemni, Angenot, Khouri, Derriennic, Dion, Bertrand, and others, whose work filled its pages, had the avowed objective of rebutting the nationalist politicians and intellectuals, particularly the sovereigntists. To be sure, this focus in no way detracts from the journal. The new *Cité libre* was important in the Quebec landscape of ideas, for its very presence confirmed the ideological pluralism of Quebec society.

As I mentioned earlier, the argument that a single orthodoxy reigns over Quebec with an iron fist seems preposterous to me. There are at present too many articulate anti-nationalist intellectuals, activists, politicians, and other citizens for the assertion that a quiet despotism exists in Quebec to be believable. In the next section, I shall explore some of their writings.

Jean-Pierre Derriennic:
An Anti-nationalist Liberal Ontology

The political scientist Jean-Pierre Derriennic is the author of a book published in 1995 that put more than one Quebec sovereigntist in a difficult position. It is easy to see why: his *Réflexion sur les illusions des indépendantistes québécois* is packed with rigorous, historically solid arguments.[34] And his students at Université Laval know how persuasive his arguments can be, whether or not they agree with them. Like Trudeau, Derriennic believes that nationalism offers little sustenance for the mind. From the very first sentence of the book, using terms that seem to be intended as general in scope, he argues that "nationalism feeds on plain truths, not reasons. It responds to objections with jocular rebuffs or arguments from authority."[35] Despite appearances, however, Derriennic is not much given to polemics. Unlike Marc Angenot, for example, he recognizes that most Quebec nationalists are democrats, and that where "the French-Canadian nationalism of the past was identity-centred ... the Quebec nationalism of today has become civic for the majority of its adherents."[36]

One need not look far to discover the ontological prism through which Derriennic observes Quebec nationalism. Like Trudeau, he believes in the moral superiority of liberal individualism, or what Charles Taylor calls "political atomism." For Derriennic, only individuals can legitimately hold rights, and in this position he is faithful to the contractualist tradition. He conceives of national, cultural, or other communities (he makes no distinction) as pure emanations from the individual wills of the members comprising them. At their own discretion, individual holders of inalienable rights can form, maintain, and dissolve communities according to their needs. Yet Derrienic cannot be ranked with the radical individualists who think that communities do nothing but impose arbitrary impediments, constraints, and obligations on individuals. On the contrary, he readily acknowledges that communities facilitate cooperation and fraternity. They can be channellers of collective egotism, just as they can create unshakeable solidarity. Derriennic further acknowledges that community allegiances are, for the majority of individuals, fundamental bearings on the identity compass.

But what are the legal implications of this observation? Parting company with the theorists, communitarian or otherwise, who argue the importance of communities in the development of identity, Derriennic thinks that there are none. "The importance of a phenomenon must not be confounded with the necessity of instituting it in law," he writes.[37] Consequently, he is a proponent of a legal individualism "in which only individuals can be the primary subjects of law."[38] True to this precept, Derriennic seeks to dissuade Quebecers from demanding collective rights designed to ensure the persistence of a majority French-speaking distinct society in North America. He is not, at least in appearance, asking them to stop identifying with the Quebec nation, but merely to "relinquish the desire to convert this nation into a state." In Derriennic's moral and political philosophy, "nations should learn, as certain religions have learned before them, to exist as voluntary groupings: nations would not have rights; individuals would have the right to organize to defend and promote their idea of national identity; states would ignore nations and recognize only citizens.

Quebec Identity

There is no lack, in Quebec, of the talent and resources to make a nation live and prosper within such an institutional framework."[39] In this conception, citizens who share a national identity can, as part of civil society, group together to defend and promote certain aspects of that identity; but they recognize the neutrality of the state vis-à-vis particular identities, and so they agree to live in an anational state.

It is, as Derriennic allows, an individualistic conception of nations, one that fits within a neo-Kantian perspective of which John Rawls and Jürgen Habermas are today's most fervent defenders. Although the liberalisms of Rawls and Habermas differ in several ways, both may be classified as "proceduralist."[40] Here contemporary societies are seen as irremediably plural, and they must come to terms with differing visions of the good life. Ethical perspectives coexist and clash within societies virtually incapable of offering a substantive and universal definition of the common good. Consequently, the role of politics is to grant individual rights and to ensure that no societal subgroup is able to politically impose its vision of the Good. State intervention must be limited to the establishment of procedures governing the defence of individual rights and the distribution of resources. Therefore the state cannot, even with the support of the majority, legislate to guarantee the persistence of certain cultural traits. Derriennic agrees: "Just laws are not made to measure for a person or group. They may be identified by the fact that they are satisfactory to all human beings, or more precisely, to any one of them."[41] The assignment of collective rights is antithetical to the ethical and cultural pluralism that is integral to Quebec society. The role of political philosophy becomes that of constructing a culturally neutral theory of justice which can rally fellow citizens with multiple ethical and identity differences. "From this point of view," as Daniel

Anti-nationalism and Political Universalism

Weinstock notes pertinently, "minority cultures will survive or perish depending on their capacity to attract and retain members in what might be termed the free market of cultures and ideas."[42]

The existence of a nation, seen as a "voluntary grouping" in this view, is intimately linked to the will of its members to give it form in civil society. Granted, there is nothing trivial about this conception. A nation only truly exists when it is perpetually affirmed, transgressed, and reconfigured by its members. However, it is legitimate to wonder whether a minority nation can rely exclusively on the private actions of its members to ensure its survival. Can a small nation really do without legislative intervention? The example of the First Nations appears to indicate the contrary. Until very recently, successive governments in Quebec and Ottawa have oscillated between assimilationist measures and a laissez-faire approach in their relations with the aboriginal peoples; these amount to the same thing in practice, since the politics of indifference subtly grades into a policy of assimilation. The results speak for themselves: all socio-economic indicators show that the First Nations (with a few exceptions) are in the grip of extreme social anomie (poverty, violence, substance abuse and alcoholism, illiteracy, dropping out, suicide). Meanwhile, a whole generation of Native people are now realizing just how much of their cultural identity has been lost. Whereas the Native value systems and world views depend upon the transmission of wisdom and knowledge by the elders, intergenerational contact has been gravely jeopardized by a lack of intervention to support the cultural development of these communities.[43] Natives of different generations, belonging to the same nation, literally no longer speak the same language. And in fact, the cultural and economic revitalization of the First Nations underway in certain communities is not taking the path of undifferentiated universal citizenship but, rather, of struggles for collective rights that could help to secure cultural differences. Treaty negotiations, the quest for political autonomy, land and natural resources claims, the forging of economic partnerships – these make up the hard core of identity politics as they are vigorously practised by the First Nations. For most Natives, cultural renaissance, political recognition, collective rights, and self-government clearly go together.[44]

In the same vein, what would have become of the French language in Quebec without Bills 101 and 86, which, no one denies, provide legal protection for the collective rights of the francophone majority? I am not evoking apocalyptic scenarios about the imminent disappearance of French in Quebec. Even in Montreal, the language is not endangered; moreover, the current linguistic compromise, largely based on the 1988 Supreme Court decision in *Ford* v. *P.G. Québec,* seems to me the product of a thoughtful and salutary trade-off between the primacy of individual rights and the institutionalization of collective measures aimed at preserving specific linguistic or cultural characteristics.[45] But this legislative provision – a clear manifestation of a more general will to build a nation and an autonomous political community in Quebec (insofar as possible in the shadow of globalization) – sits uncomfortably within the liberal ontology of Trudeau or Derriennic. As we have seen, Derriennic does not view nations as having any rights. For example, he contends with certainty that if Quebec can invoke the right to self-determination and secession, then so can any group residing in its territory: "If the francophones of Quebec have the right to decide that they are a people distinct from the Canadian people, then the Native peoples, the residents of the Gaspé Peninsula or the West Island of Montreal, or anyone else has an equivalent right. They may decide that they are peoples distinct from the Quebec people, or that they are not peoples distinct from the Canadian people."[46] The Quebecers, even if the great majority of them are at home with a national identity congruent with the legal borders of Quebec, are not a community different in kind from the community of West Islanders (who have no investment in a national self-representation).

For my part, and like the philosopher Will Kymlicka but for different reasons, I think that nations do hold special prerogatives. They do so, not by reason of any ontological status, but simply because nations are envisioned by their members as communities free to determine their own fate. Kymlicka has striven for more than a decade to amend the language of liberalism for a better fit with the deep diversity found in contemporary societies. He argues that nations, unlike cultural communities or regional groupings, possess a right to self-determination or self-government because the former claim a distinct national identity and the latter do not.[47] This distinction is based on a dual hypothesis: first, the nation – though not the only or always the most important locus of identity – remains both a source and a fundamental focus for the development of identity; and second, the absolute neutrality of the state imperils the existence of minority nations.[48] Nationalists (for the most part non-secessionist) in Scotland, Catalonia, Chiapas, and Quebec seeking points of compatibility between globalization and cultural diversity are in perfect accord with Kymlicka on this subject.

In opposition to liberal philosophers such as Kymlicka and Weinstock (whose positions, in passing, differ on important points), anti-nationalists such as Trudeau, Derriennic, and Angenot are not interested in an ever-precarious process of reconciliation between the imperatives of liberalism and the demands of national identification. In the spirit of

Trudeau, Derriennic argues that "the phenomenon of community solidarity is very much independent of rational judgment," and that "in politically civilized societies, citizenship, not the nation, must be the supreme value."[49] Here he stands in the legislator's shoes in maintaining that only citizenship, and not nationalism, is universalizable. To reach this conclusion, one must postulate the existence of only one type of nationalism: that which is driven by the principle "to each nation its state." But as we saw in the previous chapter, this is only one (albeit an important) variety among several.

In his rationalist and individualist narrative of identity, Derriennic envisions Canada as a vast, exclusively civic nation in which citizens converge towards an undifferentiated citizenship, forming voluntary associations within civil society to defend common interests.[50] Given the shadow cast by Kant over Derriennic's work, it is surely not false to assert that for him, civic nationalism is in fact a transitory historical phenomenon that may one day give way to world citizenship. Kant's cosmopolitan ideal can be glimpsed behind this sentence in particular, which is rather casually tossed off by Derriennic: "In the last several pages, I have argued for the obligation of solidarity among fellow citizens. It is a necessary value, *which may perhaps become unnecessary when an effective world citizenship comes into being.*"[51] As we shall see with Angenot and Robin, this political universalism appears to be the necessary corollary of theoretical anti-nationalism.

Marc Angenot: Completing the Project of Modernity

Resentment forms the ideological substrate of the nineteenth- and twentieth-century nationalisms – not the chauvinisms of the great powers, of course, but that of the small national entities dragging along the memory of having been subjugated and oppressed.

Marc Angenot

Marc Angenot's tirade against the "ethnic" Québécois intellectuals in the pages of *Le Devoir* in 1996 caused convulsions among certain nationalist thinkers – and for good reason.[52] His loud, vehement critiques directed at Québécois intellectuals are not the wild assertions of an anonymous pamphleteer; he is a McGill University literature professor widely renowned for his pioneering contributions to discourse analysis and the humanities in Quebec. For this reason, his letters came in for much discussion. The crossfire, partaking as it does more of polemics and vendettas than of the exchange of ideas, is of little interest in a study of the ontologies underlying different narratives of identity. Much more fertile terrain for my purposes is Angenot's essay *Les idéologies du ressentiment*, in which he reveals his position on what he calls "neo-tribalisms" and the "contemporary identity market."[53] Yet it is a difficult exercise. As two critiques have noted, the book differs from Angenot's previous work in being riddled with attacks of questionable validity on contemporary identity politics, which is the steady object of his derision.[54] As a result, his tone has shifted, becoming more suited to a dialogue of the deaf than to reciprocal elucidation. Nevertheless, I shall not attempt to unearth any internal contradictions or logical flaws that the work may contain. The critiques articulated by Jacques Pelletier and Alain Roy are serious enough to merit a response from the author concerned. For my part, I shall try to expose the "modernist nostalgia" which, as I see it, conditions Angenot's perception of contemporary identity and nationalist movements.

He is of one mind with Trudeau and Derriennic in having no sympathy for nationalism, which he sees as a desire to build a nation timorously retrenched behind the ramparts of ethnic homogeneity: "Nationalism envisaged mainly as separatism, as a *need* for secession in order to be with one's own kind, as the fantasy of never again having to compare or judge oneself on the terrain and in the terms of one's historical adversary, according to the logic that assured the latter's victory – to get rid of this adversary, burn bridges, isolate oneself so as to be accountable, from now on, only to the People of Resentment."[55] As is evident in the epigraph to this section, Angenot sees resentment as the source, the "ideological substrate," of the nationalism of small nations. However, he obscures the reasoning that would let us work our way back to his premises. As Pelletier and Roy have observed, Angenot appears to be maintaining two mutually contradictory axioms.[56] To begin with, he puts forward the heuristically promising, if not entirely original, hypothesis that resentment is a palliative, a joyless balm applied to the wounds opened by the postmodern withering of meaning. It is a by-product of the unbearable responsibility of creating meaning, value, and truth in a disenchanted universe.[57] The resurgence of resentment is thus interpreted as one of the most important contemporary manifestations of the erosion of metanarratives and the metaphysical degradation of the world.[58] Faced with growing incredulity about the universalist myths of modernity (Reason, Science, Progress, Truth, History, the Subject), resentment, in Angenot's words, "seeks to restore fetishes, stabilities, identities."[59] In a context characterized by the erosion of ultimate markers of certainty, several theorists have reflected on the problematic nature of identity and orientation in the absence of transcendental bearings. But Angenot quickly sets this issue aside in order to take up another: "Tribalism and resentment: resentment is primary, it *welds together* the tribe whose identity/cohesion is merely the result of a collective nurturing of grievances and grudges. RESENTMENT MAKES THE TRIBE: THAT IS THE ESSENCE OF MY THESIS."[60] Introduced as a compensatory attitude, resentment becomes here an ontological substrate. Nationalism, feminism, sectarianism, masculinism, and anti-Semitism are, in Angenot's prose, united by the common denominator of resentment. Nationalism – resentful and whiny by nature – flows from the reification and nurturing of grudges about a past experienced as one of domination and alienation. The nationalism of minority nations, as a "dream of hermetism," emerges, not as a desire for emancipation and transcendency, but as retrenchment to a state of alleged victimhood.[61] Nationalism, for Angenot, is a disease of reason and the will.

Resentment is therefore both a cause and a consequence. Is this a contradiction that sheds doubt on the validity of Angenot's position, as Roy and Pelletier have contended, or merely an infelicitous and convoluted formulation? Perhaps the following position should be read between the lines: resentment, as a cowardly, snivelling attitude brought on by the end of modernity, *produces* revanchist ideologies, nationalisms, and identities. I will not attempt here to settle a dispute in which the central figure seems disinclined to participate. Instead, I will dwell on the reasoning leading Angenot to view nationalism and identity politics as phenomena steeped in resentment.

He readily admits that he feels personally antagonized by ideologies of resentment in general and by identity politics (most notably nationalism) in particular.[62] What has caused this irritation? My hypothesis – and there is nothing really provocative about it – is that Angenot, like Habermas but with less nuance, wants to finish the project of modernity. Put another way, he is trying to restore meaning to the universalist, emancipatory ideals of the Enlightenment while acknowledging the bankruptcy of metaphysics. Hence the conundrum: How to develop a theory of undifferentiated citizenship, justice, human rights, communication, and "plural universalism" in a context where only "little narratives" have the right to be heard? For the purposes of his essay, Angenot defines modernity as "that period marked by largely successful attempts to keep resentment in check, to outgrow it, or to transform it into something else," while postmodernity "is marked and defined a priori by the (short- or long-term?) retreat of theories of the universal, of history (history not as a maelstrom but as something meaningful), and by the disappearance of 'horizons of reconciliation.'"[63]

Angenot's modernist nostalgia is palpable in his judgment of the current epoch (the age of resentment). For him, the worldwide ascendancy of identity politics is the most convincing manifestation that History is regressing, that postmodernity is going in circles and running on empty. "Contemporary resentment and the triumphant recrudescence of ethnocentrism and nationalism among small nations. Swimming against the current of history, consummating modern history by means of a *regression below*," writes Angenot in his at times telegraphic style.[64] As a critical theorist, he has made it his mission to demystify the pernicious ideologies of resentment and, in so doing, to help finish the project of modernity. He defends the heritage of the Enlightenment against the rise of postmodernism, cultural relativism, and "ethnonationalism."[65] The solution, in his view, is to counter retrenchment into identity politics with an openness to the universal, with the rationality of cosmopolitanism: "Any ideology of citizenship, the universal, the universality of rules of justice, dialogue, the cosmopolitan, the uncompartmented plural, is an antidote to the resentment that will never do more than feed on particularizing grudges and see fit to shut itself up inside them."[66] Although he is categorically opposed to the granting of collective rights,[67] Angenot rejects the accusation that he is writing a requiem for cultural diversity. In fact, he leads his charge against the ideologies of resentment, and ipso facto identity politics, in the name of pluralism and "receptiveness to alterity." In a section in which he seems to be heading off potential criticism, he goes as far as to write: "I do not deny identity, the feeling of identity and belonging, as a sort of (rather vague and undefined) anthropological need, but I distinguish between identity as conceived through interaction with the Other, as a becoming (as a desire for emancipation), and identity-as-grudge-holding."[68]

Well and good, but what of the imperatives of belonging and cohabitation in a context of plurality? It must be explained to us how this "anthropological need" for identity can be satisfied in a context dominated by movement, *métissage*, integration, and concomitant affirmation of difference. Angenot has nothing to say about this question since he would have all identity politics "resentful" by nature, condemned before the tribunal of a "plural universalism" about which we are told nothing. Moreover, it is revealing that he has never – no more than Derriennic, Khouri, or Robin – engaged in dialogue with internationally renowned Canadian political philosophers such as Taylor, Tully, and Kymlicka, who have theorized subjects such as rootedness, belonging, the domination of liberal values, the need for recognition, cultural hybridity, and globalization.[69] But these theories offer no great succour to Angenot, partaking as they do of all the nuances and tensions on which identity politics are constructed. Between revanchism and the will to emancipation, between openness to alterity and the need for recognition, identity politics is far from monosemous. All in all, it is hard to see how Angenot's thought can be of use in erecting ramparts against the global homogenization of cultural identities.

Quebec Identity

Régine Robin: Defetishizing Identity

> What anguish some afternoons. *Québécitude*. Quebecness. I am other. I do not belong to this "we" so often used here, even in the ads. "We." "You." "We should talk to each other." "We're at home here." Another history – the inescapable strangeness.
>
> Régine Robin

Régine Robin, writer and sociology professor at the Université du Québec à Montréal, is a distinguished intellectual figure in Quebec. Working within an unabashedly interdisciplinary theoretical approach, she has authored numerous essays and scientific works of richness and originality. Given her enviable academic reputation, her critiques of Quebec nationalism have justly given pause to the nationalist intellectuals – and all the more so in that her writing style is typically less polemical than, say, Angenot's. "Typically," since Robin too at times takes up the critique of the single orthodoxy and soft totalitarianism allegedly reigning over Quebec. In so doing, she in turn sings the song of Quebec's cultural mediocrity (see chapter 2), changing the refrain somewhat. Thus, for example, she does not hesitate to posit a more or less causal relationship between the absence of critical space, the poverty of ideas, and the hegemony of the nationalist discourse:

> Since 1979–80, what has changed on the cultural front? Everything and nothing, and it's all gotten worse. Let's not mince words; for a dissident, QUEBEC HAS BECOME UNBREATHABLE, ideologically and culturally. It is not easy to go against the grain, to think "something different," to think at all. What is lacking today is a public space for debate, for confrontation of ideas without immediately being disqualified on the grounds that we

come from somewhere else, we don't conform, or we think differently ... Only one thing has not changed: the poverty of ideas, the marginalization and exclusion of everything that was really alive and kicking and thinking differently, the poverty of critical thought, with some exceptions, naturally ... Of course, the mental space is totally taken up by political and/or cultural nationalism, by an obsession with and a fetishization of language, which, be it said, goes hand in hand with the sorry state of it.[70]

Here again, working our way back to the premises is not straightforward. It seems hard to deny the polyphony of voices and ideas, hence the existence of a critical space, in Quebec. Granted, each Quebec intellectual must personally come to terms with the nationalist challenge. However, I think the first three chapters of this essay make clear that Quebec intellectuals, as a heterogeneous group, have reacted to this challenge in very different ways. Where Cantin reaffirms Quebec neo-nationalism, Laforest critiques and proposes a new language for it, while Derriennic disputes the validity of nationalism itself. All these voices are legitimate, and above the din of polemics and wars of words, they gain in rigour and intelligibility by drawing and building on one another.

In my view, Robin makes her greatest contribution to transforming Quebec identity representations when she devotes herself to unmasking the varieties of exclusion instigated by a certain kind of nationalist discourse. She has done as much as anyone in Quebec to make the plural, shifting, elusive nature of identities intelligible. In attempting to determine what becomes of identities in a postmodern world, she finds them to be ontologically plural, fragmented, and fleeting.[71] Prior to and beyond discourse, real life is pervaded by "plural, multiple identities," by the "fragmentation of identities," and by the "choice of identities à la carte."[72] Freedom, for Robin, is embodied in non-coincidence, extrication, uprooting, farewells, disorientation (*dépaysement*), *unheimlich*. Communities are asphyxiated by the freezing and pinning down (*épinglage*) of identities, while "only disengagement, multiple allegiance, and the in-between offer room to move, breathable space."[73]

This is the perspective that Robin brings to the Quebec literary text and social discourse, where she repeatedly discovers slips of the tongue and pen evidencing a "discourse of homogeneity" and a "nostalgia for an imaginary *Gemeinschaft*."[74] Robin justly speaks out against attempts to reify or essentialize certain elements of *québécitude,* and she objects in other terms to substantialist definitions of the Québécois identity. For example, she deplores the fact that identity is too often perceived here as "an essence, an a priori datum arising from the Frenchness of the original inhabitants and their language. Language and identity coincide, as do language, identity, and culture. And so the state, the nation-state (more precisely a *volksgeist*-state) under construction, or the existing welfare state is obligated to take charge of this coincidence, this figure of totality and exclusivity, and to preserve, reflect, and reinforce it."[75] But this whole coincidence, which forms a kind of "identity flypaper," can only be presumed of those who possess a common language, identity, and culture and who share, in Robin's felicitous phrase, the same "novel of historical memory" (*roman mémoriel*).[76] That is, she asserts that contemporary Québécois identity is only accessible to the imagined French-Canadian community. Shorn of its civic trappings, Quebec nationalism is a project directed exclusively at the "original" Québécois. In this conception, the boundaries of Québécois authenticity coincide with the contours of the old French-Canadian

Anti-nationalism and Political Universalism

nation. Though a citizen of Quebec, the Other, the different, will never be truly Québécois; hence the presumed impossibility of a "plural Quebec."

In my exploration of the work of the melancholy intellectuals in chapter 1, I showed that certain nationalist authors experience the history of Quebec as being laden with trauma. According to Robin, the agenda of these intellectuals "currently excludes all those who cannot carry this weight of memory and oppression, of humiliation and memories taken from the Québécois novel of historical memory."[77] The main character of her novel *The Wanderer* is one such person. She has always felt marginalized, stigmatized, at times simply excluded; sometimes she is given a welcome, yet she remains the symbol of intriguing foreignness. "I am not from here. One doesn't become Québécois," she sighs more than once in the story.[78] The narrator is charmed by certain aspects of Quebec and wishes to explore the distinctness of its identity, but a malaise inhabits her. She might even vote Yes in the referendum (of 1980), were it not for that fear shooting through her:

> The fear of homogeneity
> of unanimity
> of the Us that excludes all others
> of the pure
> she the immigrant
> different
> deviant.
> She would hesitate.
> Because there could also be a Québécois way of witch hunting
> Because there could also be a Québécois way of being xenophobic and anti-Semitic.
> She would hesitate. Lost in this heroic struggle
> not completely hers
> not completely other.[79]

Quebec Identity

Robin writes that, in order to put an end to the exclusion that is killing contemporary Quebec, the identity fences must be torn down. We must "make lumps in the béchamel of identity and essentialism," "emerge from ethnicity"; that is, we must "hollow out within ourselves (whatever our background may happen to be) a position of identity uncertainty, decentredness, soft identity in the sense of Vattimo, displacement, deconstruction."[80] A whole labour of identity defetishization, of changing our ways of looking and thinking, of delayering and memory relandscaping, must be accomplished in order to transform the possibilities for identity in Quebec. For Robin, literature and critical thinking appear to be the tools with which to do this decentring work. However, this different relationship to the self carries with it a political agenda as well: the creation of a "new universalism." It is here that Robin, perhaps unwittingly, falls in line with the other authors studied in this chapter.

It should be said that there is nothing straightforward about reasoning from the critical to the political, and a plethora of intellectuals have stumbled over this transition. Therefore Robin should not be overly taken to task for her relative silence on the subject. Yet it is legitimate to wonder how her problematization of identity ought to transform our understanding of community and shared belonging. On the one hand, the writer and literary theorist appears to be pleading for the "imaginary homeland" – the one founded on transculturalism and respect for alterity; mental and emotional exile as norm. From this standpoint, the community becomes a non-space but never a locus of identity.[81] On the other hand, the sociologist calls for the creation of a "civic citizenship based not on origins but a shared vision of society."[82] None of this is condemnable. Moreover, as we shall see in the next chapter, this kind of citizenship already exists

Anti-nationalism and Political Universalism

in Quebec. Like Robin, I shall try to show how communities are disparate and dissensual spaces in which plural authenticities cohabit. Nevertheless, it is worth asking Robin what she has to propose to those who want to guarantee the survival of a majority francophone, pluralist nation and political community in North America, and who consequently insist on having Quebec recognized as such. At a time when consensualism in politics is having a rough time[83] – not, by the way, a deplorable state of affairs – this struggle for cultural diversity is perhaps one of the few visions of society or horizons of convergence rightly desired by Robin. She is no doubt in good faith when she writes that we must now develop a "vision that abandons the yearning for fusion in favour of a new philosophy of sharing equidistant between the romantic neo-Herderism that still haunts Quebec and the neo-liberal consumerist ideology currently serving as a model; equidistant between a return to 'us versus them' and postmodern fragmentation."[84] However, as with Derriennic and Angenot, one searches in vain through the prolegomena of her thinking on citizenship for anything that would enable Quebec to avoid cultural homogenization. "In a hostile, ghettoizing world, one must firmly counter the problematics of difference with the problematics of alterity, to be theorized within the framework of a new universalism."[85] The respect for alterity evoked by Robin is no doubt essential, but it is not clear that her ideal of undifferentiated civic citizenship can truly frame and guarantee this respect. Therefore it is incumbent upon her to specify the terms of this "new universalism."

The critique of nationalism often, through a semantic shift, ends in a plea for a universalist, cosmopolitan ideal. This shift can be found, to different degrees and in different formulations, in all the authors studied in this chapter. But if the anti-nationalists have helped to reveal the identity suffocation created by one strand of nationalist discourse, they too, it seems to me, try to lock up Quebec identities within hermetic, mutually exclusive categories. In a surprising reversal, anti-nationalism finds itself afflicted with the evil it denounces: the "pinning down" of identity, in Robin's phrase. By voluntarily or inadvertently blocking access to a common collective identity, the anti-nationalists bind the people of Quebec to a cosmopolitan identity that makes fragile the cultural and intersubjective space necessary for the development of a plural and distinct identity – an identity that resists the comforts of Jacobin homogeneity but stands up to the forces attempting to level cultural differences in the world. As I shall strive to demonstrate in the last chapter of this book, "exclusivist" nationalisms and cosmopolitanisms are of a piece. If it is the theorist's job to reveal the exclusions created and maintained by certain discourses, practices, or institutions, it is not his or her job to order individuals' loyalties, allegiances, and horizons of meaning.

4

From Identity to Democracy: Quebec and the Challenge of Pluralism

The Quebec social imaginary, as we have seen, is besieged by identity representations drawn from melancholy nationalism and cosmopolitanism anti-nationalism. However, these two paradigmatic codes do not exhaust the possibilities. Other voices are speaking up to worry, problematize, throw a wrench into, this perennial opposition. Besides Laforest and Létourneau, intellectuals and writers such as Sherry Simon, Pierre Nepveu, Marco Micone, Monique LaRue, Mikhaël Elbaz, Simon Harel, Danielle Juteau, and Daniel Salée, to name just a few, all think and talk about Quebec outside the nationalism-anti-nationalism dichotomy. Quebec is increasingly being told as a dissensual, plural community of conversation in which different narratives tolerate, hybridize, and intermingle with one another, without thereby being tagged as inauthentic.[1] I shall devote the first part of this chapter to defining the plural, hybrid nature of contemporary cultural identities. In the second part, I shall bring these theoretical considerations to bear on the context of contemporary Quebec.

Quebec Identity

DIALOGICAL SPACES AND HORIZONS OF MEANING: NATIONS AND CULTURES IN OUR TIME

As I observed in my introduction, identity has become the object of heated debate, both in theoretical contexts and in political praxis. In books and public forums, monist and pluralist perspectives on identity confront and respond to one another.[2] Even if one can only agree with Stuart Hall that identities, once deconstructed, "cannot be thought in the old way,"[3] this does not mean that exclusivist and substantialist conceptions and practices have given up the ghost. Nevertheless, essentialist perspectives – that is, approaches which elide the historicity of identities and attempt to pin an immutable substance, "fibre," or authenticity to them – have to confront a plethora of non-essentialist, constructivist viewpoints. What is more, in the last thirty years, while the Marxist fascination with social class has been enriched (not replaced) by other issues such as gender, sexual identity, and ethnicity;[4] while liberalism has been increasingly unable to hide behind a sham political neutrality; and while nationalism has been transgressed from within and without, struggles for recognition and political autonomy waged by minority cultures and groups have become an important vector of democratic transformation.

Since the nineteenth century, the nation has been the most powerful source of collective identification, and for that reason, nationalism as a relationship to self and others differs from other modern political ideologies. Benedict Anderson, in his classic study, suggests that nationalism is a social signifier whose role is to guarantee the continuity of an imagined community over time and space; as such, it is closer in spirit to religion than to political ideology.[5] Even in an age of globalization and of radical political and economic integration, formerly oppressed nations continue to struggle for identity recognition and a degree of political autonomy. This phenomenon leads Craig Calhoun to assert, with justification, that national identity has nearly always been perceived as more important and categorical than other identities of the modern subject.[6] But what thinkers such as Anderson and Homi Bhabha call "the homogeneous empty time" of nations has now been disrupted. According to Bhabha, the writing of the nation emerges from the fissure between the "continuist, accumulative temporality" of nationalism (the pedagogical) and the constant reformulation and transgression of this historical narrative in the present (the performative).[7] He argues that there is a lag between the story told about the nation in order to give it a degree of coherence and the appropriation of that story by the people and groups of which the nation is composed. Hence the nation is the product of a complex dynamic between the writing or narration of the collective experience and the enunciation of this same experience by individual and collective subjects in the present.

It is now widely accepted, though, that individuals enjoy a plurality of identity spaces. It is no longer self-evident – perhaps it never was – that nationality can be considered an all-encompassing collective identity capable of ordering the citizen's other allegiances and identifications.[8] Without underestimating the importance of national identities, it has become impossible to take for granted that nationality necessarily stands prior to other identity referents such as ethnicity, gender, sexual identity, and class. In this period of late modernity, nationality is only one (albeit an important) source of collective identification among others. Since the borders of cultural and national identities are not always congruent (as a result of the multicultural or polyethnic nature of contemporary nation-states), I shall begin by attempting to grasp the meaning of cultural identity in an age of movement and diversity.

As cultural agents, subjects make their way and evolve in and through cultures that are not static, immutable codes but, rather, dynamic and evolving processes. Cultures are not the homogeneous spaces described by certain communitarian thinkers, in which agents "discover" their identity by deepening their awareness of their community; they are "strange multiplicities" in which identities are made, unmade, and remade. As Simon suggests, "culture is not a comfortable wrapper, a reassuring source of immediate signification, but a set of discourses and practices competing on a symbolic playing field."[9] A culture is a plural, intersubjective site that produces meaning and possibilities for disclosure, potential recognition, disorientation, and, despite everything, a collective self-consciousness. Or as Tully puts it:

Cultures are not internally homogeneous. They are continuously contested, imagined and reimagined, transformed and negotiated, both by their members and through their interaction with others. The identity, and so the meaning, of any culture is thus aspectival rather than essential [it varies depending on the angle from which it is viewed]: like many complex human phenomena, such as language and games, cultural identity changes as it is approached from different paths and a variety of aspects come into view. Cultural diversity is a tangled labyrinth of intertwining cultural differences *and* similarities, not a panopticon of fixed, independent and incommensurable worldviews in which we are either prisoners or cosmopolitan spectators in the central tower.[10]

The 1990s witnessed an extraordinary flowering of research on the hybrid nature of cultural identities. Using language similar to Simon and Tully, the anthropologist James Clifford claims that a culture is "a multiply authored invention, ... a shifting paradox, an ongoing translation, ... a nonconsensual negotiation of contrastive identity."[11] Cultures are constituted relationally from within and without, and through a process of appropriation/translation, and as a result, the "different" is found both inside and outside identities. Difference is at once intrinsic and extrinsic to each community. This trace of difference at the heart of identity has largely been thematized by thinkers influenced more or less directly by post-structuralism. The competing modernist interpretation of difference – nowhere more patent than in the work of Thomas Hobbes – considers it to be that which is external to the self. Identity is constituted in opposition to a necessarily reified difference. On this model, oppositions of subject-object, us-them, inside-outside, or friend-enemy are constructed as hermetic, mutually exclusive dichotomies; and the stabilization of self-integrity, its preservation, depends on constant reiteration of this supposedly ontological difference between self and other.[12] The creation of homogeneous identity necessitates the hypothesis of a radically heterogeneous, and therefore threatening, exterior.[13]

Perhaps the most revealing exemplification of this process of identity production/reproduction through reification of the Other is the phenomenon of "orientalism" described by Edward Said. The orientalists, in their "imaginative demonology of 'the mysterious Orient,'" postulated the existence of an ontological and epistemological difference between Occident (the familiar) and Orient (the strange).[14] In his book *Orientalism*, Said tries to show that "European culture gained in strength and identity by setting itself off against the Orient as a sort of surrogate and even underground self."[15] Moreover, "what gave the Oriental's world its intelligibility and identity was not the result of his own efforts but rather the whole complex series of knowledgeable manipulations by which the Orient was identified by the West."[16]

A refined version of the modernist interpretation of difference may be found in the Hegelian dialectic. In Hegel's political philosophy, or one interpretation thereof, the stage of "abstract right" (when the subject denies and invalidates the essence granted to her or him a priori) and the stage of "subjective morality" (in which the abstract will takes on a content through its encounter with other subjectivities) are reconciled at the stage of "synthesis" or "objective morality," the final moment of the dialectic.[17] In this way, difference dissolves into identity; or put another way, identity and difference are engulfed in a new synthetic identity. Of course, the dialectic never attains a resting state; it is never frozen in History; the process is continuous. However, as I shall indicate below, there is in Hegel's dialectic a moment of reconciliation when different subjectivities come to fully recognize one another in a conception of the ethical life. In any case, the point here is not to go into the details of Hegel's philosophy of right but, rather, to show how classical political philosophy dealt with the concept of difference. And indeed, we see that either identity is fashioned and maintained in opposition to an objectified difference (Hobbes) or it absorbs difference (Hegel); but in both cases, difference withers and vanishes.

Now that numerous authors have attempted to deconstruct the binary opposition between self and other, it seems possible to think differently about difference. Simply put, it is endogenous to identity. Difference is not necessarily completely dissolved, but neither can it always be decanted from identity. This is why Stuart Hall considers contact and interaction with difference to be necessary conditions for the creation of identity: "Identities are constructed through, not outside, difference."[18] This irreducible trace of alterity at the core of identity helps us to understand what is at first sight a sibylline phrase of Jacques Derrida to the effect that identities are not completely identical to themselves. In Derrida's words: "*What is proper to a culture is to not be identical to itself.* Not to not have an identity, but not to be able to identify itself, to be able to say 'me' or 'we'; to be able to take the form of a subject only in the non-identity to itself or, if you prefer, only in the difference *with itself* [*avec soi*]. There is no culture or cultural identity without this difference *with itself*. In this case, self-difference, difference to itself [*différence à soi*], that which differs and diverges from itself, of itself, would also be the *difference (from) with itself* [*différence (d')avec soi*], a difference at once internal and irreducible to the 'at home (with itself).'"[19]

By becoming aware of the heterogeneous nature of cultural identities, we unearth the borrowings, the exchanges, the translations – the fissures – that constitute our own identity. We thereby disqualify all identity or recognition politics based on claims of homogeneity or cultural purity. Indeed, as Bhabha pertinently suggests, identities are not transparent.[20] Identity narratives emanate from conscious and unconscious dialogues with the Other, who also finds him or herself both inside and outside cultural identities. Identities take shape in the interpretation of an evolving, evanescent experience whose contours cannot be totally delimited. But in contrast to the assertions of a certain type of postmodernism, this interpretive sketching does not culminate in the relativist assertion that cultures are incommensurable, which would render all inter- or transcultural dialogue impossible.

On the contrary, the "Other" is perceived here as a complex arrangement of differences *and* similarities, not a locus of pure opacity and alterity. In this way, culture, nation, and other loci of identity can be theorized as spaces of plurivocal, dissensual dialogue.

What post-colonialist authors term the "diasporic experience" can help us to comprehend the pluralization of cultural identities and the dissemination of communities of conversation. In making a trope of the diasporic experience, it is not these authors' intention to trivialize the history, the historical singularities, of different diasporas. Each diaspora is a repository of a particular set of historical experiences, and it is extremely difficult to produce a comprehensive diaspora theory that applies to every spatiotemporal context. Instead, the diasporic experience refers to a feeling of disorientation not alien, at least in principle, to national political subjects who live with difference as part of their culture of origin. Diasporic identities, composed of both "roots and routes," complicate the intuitive association between space and community. By entertaining complex relations with both the community of origin and the host country, diasporic subjectivities help us imagine how people can create new instances of "us" without necessarily sharing the same territory. According to Clifford (citing Joseph Rouse), diasporic relations and webs exemplify how "[s]eparate places become effectively a single community 'through the continuous circulation of people, money, goods, and information.'"[21] Therefore Josée Bergeron is right when she argues for the recognition that "if identities can be superimposed, spaces can too. One can be situated in several spaces at the same time."[22] A person can belong at the same time to, say, the Montreal Italian community (and so entertain complex and specific relations with Italy, Quebec, and Canada), a transnational environmental movement, a virtual community, and various local networks, while still defining her or himself as a "world citizen" (to use the stock expression). The priority given to these affiliations may change over time; fullness, for some, may be embodied precisely in the maintenance of a delicate balance among identifications that are by turns convergent or contradictory. It is no longer the job of political philosophy to build a hierarchy of communities of belonging for the contemporary subject. And monist discourse, whether it be Marxist, nationalist, ethnicist, or cosmopolitanist, no longer suffices to articulate the lived experience of subjects/citizens living their lives within such identity webs. In fact, diasporic identities offer a wealth of examples of deterritorialized communities, whose existence renders such totalizing collective identities highly problematic. Diasporic identities are hard to reconcile with the discourses of cultural purity upheld by certain nationalist leaders, and equally so with liberal neutrality; they encourage the formation of plural, differentiated (Iris Marion Young) and non-absolutist (Clifford) citizenships.

In short, both diasporic and national subjects potentially bear multiple identities and operate – to differing degrees and under unequal socio-economic conditions – within heterogeneous communities. Difference exudes from the very pores of culture, and the sources of personal identity are multiple and disseminated. One conclusion we must draw is that there can be no perfect coincidence between part and whole or between individual and community; for the multiplicity of identity codes integral to individuals causes organic conceptions of communities to implode. To take an example, people of the same gender and nationality may feel partially alien to one another as a result of their sexual identity or antinomic political affiliations. Even within the (shifting) boundaries of a single collective identity, such as the "French-Canadian" identity of the past, people's relationships to the past and future are too diverse for this "we" to speak in unison. Political and cultural spaces are the effect of a variety of narrative and identity trajectories. The experience of "cultural diffraction" described by Simon is not at all limited to migrants; it is lived and experienced within national cultures themselves. Cultures are ambivalent sites configured by encounters among different authenticities. This is why it is becoming increasingly difficult to say "we" or, echoing Fernand Dumont, to come up with "common reasons" in an era of diversity.

Tzvetan Todorov's self-description as a "stateless man" (*homme dépaysé*) may also serve as a trope to illustrate the potential for surprise/disorientation that contemporary subjects can experience, even at home. The phenomenon of transculturation discussed by Todorov is experienced by migrants acquiring and assimilating the identity codes of their new culture without casting off their original cultural identity. But it is also experienced by national subjects belonging to different imagined communities and living with difference at home. According to the anthropologist Arjun Appadurai, because of mass migration and the globalization of means of communication, people now live in various "imagined worlds," that is, "the multiple worlds that are constituted by the historically situated imaginations of persons and groups spread around the globe."[23] However, being disoriented does not imply that one (necessarily) feels like a stranger in his or her own country. It means that compatriots can live the same national reality at different levels, following different rhythms. As we saw with Tully, subjects approach their culture from a plurality of perspectives that highlight the various constitutive aspects of their cultural identity.

Identities disclose different sides of themselves, depending on the angle from which they are interpreted. Bhabha probably has this latent ambivalence in mind in his constant references to the phenomena of "liminality," "third space," and "in-between." One finds in Bhabha the idea that subjects belonging to the same nation do not always have the same "present," and this inevitably vexes their sense of contemporaneity.[24] As Clifford suggests, no one can be an insider to all spheres and dimensions of her or his community. In reality, contemporary subjects are disoriented, since they are frequently surprised and troubled by the complexity of their own identity, those of their fellow beings, and those of the communities to which they belong. Identity, understood from a non-Hegelian point of view, surpasses our capacity for synthesis.[25]

It has in fact become increasingly difficult to conceptualize the national community from a Hegelian standpoint. The subject, for Hegel, is not a monad or an atom. Subjects can only gain intelligence of themselves and actualize their different roles by committing to an ethical order that transcends their own subjectivity. Considering Kant's categorical imperative to be an "empty formalism," Hegel believed that only by meeting a set of moral obligations defined by their community can subjects give a substance and an orientation to their practical reason. These duties form what he called "the ethical life" (*Sittlichkeit*). As Charles Taylor reminds us, the term "*Sittlichkeit* refers to the moral obligations I have to an ongoing community of which I am part ... It is in virtue of its being an ongoing affair that I have these obligations; and my fulfillment of these obligations is what sustains it and keeps it in being."[26] The ethical life, embodied in the state, is composed of the norms, customs, traditions, and institutions of a given political community. Simply stated, subjects actualize their freedom by fulfilling their duties and adhering to the norms they themselves have contributed to building through the exercise of their subjective will (the first moment of the dialectic). Although there are paragraphs in *Principles of the Philosophy of Right* that may raise the hackles of certain liberal thinkers, the Hegelian state is not despotic; it is a place of reconciliation or synthesis between individual freedom and the obligations inherent to life in society.

But this reconciliation is precisely what is impeded by the process of pluralization of identities described in this chapter. Taylor maintains that in Hegel "the set of practices and institutions which make up the public life of the community express the most important norms, most essential to its members' identity, so that they are only sustained in their identity by their participation in these practices and institutions."[27] Since identity, in the final analysis, depends on the observance of these rules and norms, subjects must reserve their "ultimate allegiance" for the primary, indispensable space: the political community.[28] However, it is quite possible for contemporary subjects, who are in many cases disoriented and attempting to accommodate contradictory affiliations, to feel suffocated within an organic conception of the community such as Hegel's. It seems more promising to view the community as a site of deliberation and articulation, not one of fusion. As a corollary, we must reject the idea that the survival and stability of a community ultimately depend on a set of convergent, consensual values. Of course, certain common reasons do correspond to each period in the history of a community; but in the long run it is as agonistic sites of narration, disclosure, deliberation, potential recognition, and dissent that communities remain essential identity spaces. In other words, communities – which are not limited to nation and ethnicity, but obviously include these two types of collective identity – are plurivocal, and hence dissensual, "communities of conversation."

Therefore what needs to be criticized in the Hegelian conception of community (a conception rearticulated by several contemporary theorists of the nation) is not the idea that community is indispensable to the development of identity. The practices of developing and forming an identity are dialogical, or intersubjective. Intersubjectivity does not arise exclusively out of deliberate interactions between self-interested, rational, disengaged agents. Identity, as an interpretive narrative, can only emerge from the sharing of a vocabulary and the confrontation of views on this shared world. The hermeneutics of the self requires dialogue with the Other; identity is dialogical prior to being monological. It is by evolving within "webs of interlocution," in Taylor's phrase, that contemporary subjects develop the interactions necessary to the maintenance and flourishing of a personal identity which finds increasingly scarce confirmation from metanarrative or transcendental sources of identity. With the secularization of the world, the last ramparts of identity are crumbling.

What is questionable, then, in the Hegelian and neo-Hegelian conceptions is their propensity to create a hierarchy of personal allegiances and loyalties. Specifically, such a hierarchy does not follow, as some theorists are led to claim, from the undeniably fundamental importance of national identity in the development of personal identity; from the fact that it offers subjects a language, one or more histories, a groundedness from which to apprehend the world. For example, Daniel Jacques, in his cautious and moderate defence of the nation, argues that the philosopher's job is to "order" the multiple affiliations of the contemporary subject: "It is not at all a matter of denying the existence of a plurality of allegiances in modern societies, much less reducing them to an imaginary unity, but at best *ordering* this inescapable diversity in such a way as to avoid contradiction."[29] Jacques accepts identity and moral pluralism insofar as it does not challenge the predominance of national identification. In *Nationalité et modernité* he ties the fate of the freedom of the moderns to that of the nation. He argues that the nation remains, at this particular moment in our history,[30] the most appropriate arena for political action and the most important site of recognition for contemporary subjects. If so, then the nation "should not be seen as one of several attachments, as a community surrounded by a myriad of other communities within a multicultural state."[31]

Yet it is becoming increasingly obvious that if the nation remains for many a vital structure for disclosure and recognition, a plethora of other identity sites are challenging its monopoly. Gender, sexual identity, ethnicity, social class, new social movements, generational positioning, and virtual communities are all identity referents and sites of political involvement that coexist with and rival nationality. It is time for us to acknowledge that the intersubjective spaces and communities of conversation necessary to the forging of identity are plural and dispersed; that subjects may act politically in many different spheres. Michel Venne and Daniel Jacques must show us how and why, in the era of new social movements and the proliferation of political identities, the nation is "the only strictly political space left to us."[32] In fact, it is not always the best – and rarely the only – possible and desirable political demarcation. Moreover, dilemmas and conflicts often arise among these multiple allegiances. A Native woman living in Canada, for example, can be simultaneously fighting against machismo, and hence for the application of the Charter of Rights and Freedoms within her community, and neo-colonialism, and hence for the right of Native peoples to self-determination and self-government.[33] As Foucault suggests, what we are and what we want change according to the problems we face, and they fluctuate in step with the peregrinations of our identity.[34] It is up to subjects themselves to order loyalties and attachments that may turn out to be irreconcilable. Within the conceptual framework outlined in this essay, freedom resides in the possibility for self-disclosure, deliberation, and dissent within a plurality of intersubjective spheres, the nation obviously being one of them.[35]

My insistence on the disorientation that a subject can experience even within his or her culture of origin and the "desacralization" of the nation do not necessarily imply a plea for post-national identities. I am not writing an ode to displacement, acculturation, or perpetual rootlessness. On the contrary, this insistence invites us to see movement, plurality, and tension as *potential* figures of contemporary identity. It has the further effect of drawing our attention to the great polyphony and complexity that may be found in the origins, memories, and aspirations shared by people with a common identity. At issue here is not a new "patriotism" towards identity ambiguity[36] but, rather, a recognition that there can be movement and non-coincidence even in people who have (more or less freely) chosen staticity, and whose identities appear to be entire, stable, and readily discernible. Thus Clifford, despite his determination to exhibit the complexity of the aboriginal identities observed by ethnologists, refuses to consider his work as "nomadology": "My point, again, is not simply to invert the strategies of cultural localization, the making of 'natives,' which I criticized at the outset. I'm not saying there are no locales or homes, that everyone is – or should be – traveling, or cosmopolitan, or deterritorialized. This is not nomadology. Rather, what is at stake is a comparative cultural studies approach to specific histories, tactics, everyday practices of dwelling *and* traveling: traveling-in-dwelling, dwelling-in-traveling."[37]

Authenticity, then, cannot be envisaged as a perfect match between subject and culture. It is inevitably a plural construct, for there is more than one way to be an authentic subject.[38] The political sphere can certainly endow citizenship with content, but authenticity, linked to the much broader domain of identity, cannot be defined in substantive terms. It is in this new context that critical thinking about identity takes on such great practical importance. Reminding ourselves that identity is fashioned from the stuff of difference can help to perforate the boundaries of authenticity. The thoughtful articulation of the ambivalence that potentially sits at the heart of individual and collective identities can enable us to "politicize naturalized identities;"[39] or to perceive what is contingent in identities taken to be necessary.[40] This awareness of the origins of identity can give rise to an "ethical sensitivity" to difference, ensuring that the Other is not demonized or annihilated; and what is more, it can provide the foundation for a new political identity based on respect for alterity and recognition of the heterogeneity of the shared culture. For Tully, deliberation and debate on the different faces of authenticity can "foster a new, shared identity among the interlocutors: an identity that consists in the awareness of and respect for the diversity of respectworthy identities of their fellow citizens and of the place of one's own identity among the diversity of overlapping identities ... This shared identity of diversity awareness is precisely the citizen identity appropriate to, and capable of holding together, multicultural and multinational political associations."[41] In sum, a plurality of authenticities meet and interpenetrate on the public square, perpetually recreating the distinctness of a shared cultural identity. A by-product is a new political identity built out of respect for alternative or even contradictory narratives of identity, which can emerge from this dialogue held under human – all too human – conditions.

As we have seen, this reconceptualization of cultural identities and communities of conversation is incompatible with exclusivist cosmopolitan and nationalist ontologies. This ethical sensitivity to the Other certainly leads to a critique of neo-imperialist efforts to impose cultural homogeneity and purity, but it does not cloak an implicit apology for post-national identities. If the "at home" can no longer be conceived of as a place of comfort perfectly identical to itself, this does not mean that a subject will experience the same degree of disorientation anywhere in the world. The cosmopolitanist postulate to the effect that human beings inhabit reason first and any particular culture accessorily is not proof against anti-essentialist arguments. The nation remains vital for many as an intersubjective sphere, an agora, and an identity horizon. In addition, it is entirely possible to feel deeply attached to one's culture (or at any rate one's vision of it), and especially to its future prospects, yet maintain an agonistic relationship with it. Being nationalist in the (very) broad, non-standard sense of the term – that is, feeling attached to one's national identity and being driven by a desire to promote it – does not imply that this allegiance supplants all others, that the universal is perpetually sacrificed on the altar of the particular. In this context, the diasporic experience can allow us to conceive of the "at home" neither as a perfect place of coincidence nor as a futile myth, but as the indispensable nexus among plural, disparate allegiances. In my concluding remarks, I shall attempt to theorize Quebec in these terms.

BETWEEN COMFORT AND INDIFFERENCE:
IDENTITY IN QUEBEC[42]

Critical ontology, as a philosophical attitude and practice of self, can serve to historicize various sacralized fragments of identity, to situate and relativize our narratives of identity, and to problematize representations of ourselves that have become calcified over time. In so doing, it can help us to free ourselves from ourselves, to become other. My goal in addressing the issues of identity in Quebec from this perspective has been to explore certain representations that have served, and still serve, to name that identity, and I am now in a position to outline some alternative figures of ourselves. Even though an increasing number of narrators are involved in writing a plural Quebec authenticity whose boundaries are porous, the collective imagination of Quebecers remains largely occupied by the perennial confrontation between melancholy nationalism and universalist anti-nationalism. My aim in writing this book has obviously not been to try to eradicate these two paradigmatic narratives, but I want to bring them into the agora, to confront them with other narratives that I see as less exclusive and providing a better fit with the contemporary Quebec experience. And these new narratives, too, will have to be revisited, critiqued, and remade. This whole chapter, in fact, might be regarded as "biodegradable." It will have to be rewritten from time to time in the light of new and evolving "ecologies" of the Quebec reality (in Nepveu's lovely phrase).

Unlike many critics of Quebec nationalism, I think it is wrong to label this society as ethnic, closed, xenophobic, or "resentful." Quite the contrary: several studies have concluded that it is relatively open, plural, and liberal.[43] A minority of Quebec nationalists might like to see immigrants fully assimilate when they accept Quebec citizenship, but the official policies of the Quebec government are aimed at integration, not assimilation. Integration may not be a smooth or effortless process, but it does help to open up the centre, to problematize the norm. Put differently, integration invites people to defend convergent values (such as liberal values and the French language in Quebec) and to recompose the texture and parameters of identity. Difference, whether it be sexual, cultural, linguistic, gender-based, or another kind, is starting to be seen as a wellspring from which identity can draw, instead of a problem it has to solve. The expansion and fissuring of the centre is proceeding slowly, it is true, but no more slowly in Quebec than in other nominally liberal societies.

If pluralism is becoming increasingly integral to the fabric of Quebec institutions and discourses, it remains true that a sizable number of nationalists – professors, intellectuals, artists, politicians, and other citizens – believe that there is a true and authentic way to be Québécois and that the elements of that identity can be defined in substantive terms. At a certain period, many poets and intellectuals maintained that in order to be authentic, the Québécois identity had to be expressed in *joual* (dialect). As I explained in chapter 1, certain melancholy nationalists still believe deep down that the Québécois are fundamentally colonized and that the *real Québécois* must be a sovereigntist of some kind. But by objectifying the Québécois identity, we run the considerable risk of turning the Québécois into an endangered species. For indubitably, if we can define *the* substance of that identity, we can also determine who is an authentic Quebecer and who is not; and the substantive definition of "Quebec-ness" might very well disqualify each Quebecer taken individually. Thus we have Jacques Parizeau arguing that separatism constitutes the marrow of Québécois authenticity: "Feeling Québécois comes little by little. I myself was a federalist until my late thirties. I changed my mind when I realized that Quebec and Canada neutralize each other when they go head to head; they become immobile, mired in trifling conflicts. I have no quarrel with those who have decided to be Canadians. I, like many others, have chosen to be Québécois."[44] In reflecting on the results of the 1995 referendum, Parizeau goes further, concluding that "the majority of francophone Quebecers want Quebec to become a country. *They have chosen their identity and their country.* As for the non-francophone Quebecers (17 per cent the population), almost all of them voted NO."[45]

This "Quebec version of the republican identity of France" (Karmis), dominated by a particular idea of Quebec, is manifested in all spheres of Quebec society. Writings on "national" literature in the era of pluralism are highly revealing in this regard.[46] For example, the anonymous nationalist writer/"surveyor" described by Monique LaRue at a conference that gave rise to a stormy debate is trying, like many others, to canton the Québécois identity into inviolable categories. Based on the "heroic priorness" of the Québécois authors who can trace their Quebec ancestry into the distant past, this surveyor takes a new generation of immigrant writers to task for thematically and stylistically tearing down the fences around Quebec literature. He asserts that these authors are attached to their own historical memories, so they write with the distance intrinsic to migration. They are not on a "quest for identity" and do not appropriate the "web of references," the "intertextual dynamic," or the "imaginary space" specific to Quebec literature.[47] In short, the migrant writers, says the surveyor described by LaRue, are a threat to the "singularity" – read "authenticity" – of Québécois literature and, a fortiori, the Québécois identity. He is not alone in making this judgment. Father Julien Harvey, a careful and generous observer of Quebec society, takes issue with Karmis's proposition that any interpretation of the Québécois identity based on its literature must take account of writers such as Neil Bissoondath, Ying Chen, Sergio Kokis, Dany Laferrière, and Stanley Péan. For Harvey, these writers are "citizens of Quebec, but *literarily speaking*, none of them is Québécois."[48] Once it is reified, literature too can serve as a yardstick for the (in)authenticity of Quebec writers from elsewhere. Yet as Robin stresses, writers, regardless of cultural affiliation, are by their nature "stealers of myths, words, and images, smugglers of fictionalized memories."[49]

In brief, Quebec society is still traversed by a "substantialist" current that would lock up identity behind hermetic fences. Now, contrary to what its harshest critics imply, the interpretation defended by this nationalist tendency is not (or only rarely) based on criteria that would make blood and pedigree the basis of identity. It is usually based on a socially and culturally constructed ethic of authenticity to which Quebecers of all backgrounds must adhere if they want to be the genuine article.

In short, we must criticize this type of nationalism, which foments exclusion; yet this critique should not lead us to espouse the other ideological pole: anti-nationalism. As we have seen, anti-nationalism and political universalism undermine the existence of minority nations, particularly in a period of accelerated globalization. In so doing, they deprive contemporary subjects of a space for mutual disclosure and acknowledgment, a site of potential recognition, and a horizon of meaning that are fundamental for many. We must cease to view the nation as the only or necessarily the most important source of collective identification, on the one hand, or a jail cell for the identity, on the other. If, following Ernest Renan, we must see the nation as a source of omissions, illusions, and myths, we must also consider it as productive of lucidity and originality. A subject's potential for resistance and transgression does not emerge out of a vacuum.

Unlike Létourneau, I do not believe that the sole purpose of the "Quebec nation" as a concept is to refound the Québécois community through its rise to sovereignty.[50] A nation, we should remember, is an imagined community. And in fact, precisely because of the process of Quebecization of the Quebec community described by Létourneau, it happens that a large majority of francophones have come to imagine and identify with a national identity that embraces and becomes indistinguishable from the territorial borders of Quebec. While it is surely true, as he contends, that "three worlds" (francophone, anglophone, and Native) can be discerned in Quebec[51] and that many members of the latter two do not see themselves as belonging to a *Quebec* nation, it remains that a Quebec (territorial) national identity has supplanted a French-Canadian (cultural and linguistic) national identity in the minds of a vast majority of Quebec francophones. The affirmation of this new national identity in no way denies the existence of the First Nations or the anglophone national minority in Quebec. Contemporary Quebec is configured in such a way that it becomes necessary to reconceptualize the "nation" (since that is how Quebec is imagined by a substantial majority of Quebecers), without excluding the possibility of a plurality of allegiances. When represented in this way, Quebec becomes a nation respectful of the minority nations living within it, who contribute to the perpetual recreation of its distinctness in North America.

A number of observers today are indeed managing to navigate these waters, to theorize Quebec as a plurivocal, dissensual community of conversation without falling into an apology for post-national identities. My critique of the two paradigmatic interpretations of identity in Quebec and my outline of an alternative narration stand as a brief paragraph in this text being written collectively, synchronously, and non-consensually. Quebec-ness today is composed of many types of elements – past and present, cultural and intercultural, ethnic and civic, temporal and spatial, imaginary and material, local and global – and any attempt to homogenize that identity with the wider world or purify the difference within it strikes a frontal blow at the possibility of Quebecers seeing their identities as plural. To the great displeasure of certain theorists, many Quebecers have no desire to cap any of the wellsprings of their identity. Between the comfort of a tightly knit authenticity and an indifference to the shared values of the majority, a plural, labile Quebec identity is laboriously making its way. And for this reason, I consider the melancholy nationalist and universalist antinationalist conceptions discussed in this essay to be similar in kind.

Therefore, even though it is becoming increasingly difficult to enunciate convergent values on which the Quebec society of the future could be founded, one of these could be the recognition that *québécité* is a polymorphous creation. Specifically, the melancholy nationalists, without necessarily relinquishing their interpretation of Quebec's past, would accept that other authentic Quebecers do not see themselves as fitting into their unitary, teleological historical storyline. Neither would the part of the population that identifies with a specific language, historical narrative, and set of aspirations be asked to renounce these elements of their identity. Finally, Quebecers as a group would accept that the Native peoples who share the same land conceive of themselves as autonomous communities; they consider their attachment to Quebec as secondary – or even instrumental – and insist that any bilateral political negotiation be based on a relationship of nation to nation.[52]

In fact, these different Quebec authenticities that I have tried to narrate are already clashing with, tolerating, and intermingling with one another in the agora. It is time for the narrators and political leaders of Quebec to take cognizance of this exuberant activity. As I have tried to show, some of the best-known writers on the Quebec condition have difficulty coming to grips with identity pluralism. Likewise, the political imagination in both Quebec and Canada has not yet taken up the challenge of contemporary identity indeterminacy. Both the Canada of 1982 (obstinately refusing to consider itself a multinational federation) and the traditional sovereigntist project (giving no convincing signs that it can accommodate heterogeneity)[53] have yet to take seriously the complexity of identities in Quebec. Narrators and political leaders alike have failed to display the requisite modesty in dealing with the peregrinations of identity today. Perhaps this will be a challenge for future generations – not generations speaking in unison, of course, but the protagonists of a critical dialogue between generations and viewpoints; for generations, like cultures, are rarely consensual.

Some may charge that this wish is overly utopian; that there is not enough common ground among Quebec's interpreters to imagine them grouped together in such a communicative space, where each could acknowledge the other's legitimate right to speak of and for Quebec. But is this really true? Is it so difficult to accept that the neo-nationalists, through their ceaseless interpretive work, have done much to give Quebec a self-awareness based on which it is now possible to imagine Quebec differently? That from the outset, the anti-nationalists have tempered the nationalist discourse, helping to point out (and hence to combat) the exclusions inherent in a certain way of seeing and saying Quebec? That Laurendeau and his intellectual legacy have laid the groundwork for a conception of the Quebec community outside the enduring opposition between nationalism and anti-nationalism? That the First Nations leaders and the migrant writers have provided us with the materials of a truly post-imperial language? That those who conceptualize and describe a plural, hybrid Quebec are creating a narrative of identity that rather closely matches the changing faces of contemporary Quebec?

It is not a matter of Quebec's establishing a definitive consensual identity that could and should be recognized by Canada, the First Nations, and the rest of the world. This could only be done at the cost of marginalizing and excluding dissident voices. Rather than harping on the development of a definitive form of recognition or constitutional framework, our efforts might be better devoted to solidifying a democratic, dialogical ethos that can influence how the inevitable disagreements over identity representations and public policy are addressed and negotiated. Nor is it a matter of closing one's eyes to the other political moment, the moment of decision and institutionalization (the first being that of deliberation), the tragic but unavoidable moment when injustices are committed and freedoms abridged. Sooner or later, and under ever-imperfect circumstances, political decisions must be made. Among those who have taken part in the deliberations, some will contend that their rights were violated. And perhaps time will prove the dissident voices right. The telos of such democratic activity must be to ensure that it is practised with "as little domination as possible."[54] A society will be truly free if the conditions are in place for these dissidents to highlight the issues that pose a problem at the first stage of the political process (deliberation) and prevent them from becoming mired in the techno-bureaucratic apparatus which, in Quebec as elsewhere, tends to stand in for the agora.

This democratic, dialogical attitude is not lacking in Quebec; the task before us is to practise, theorize, and, in so doing, further consolidate this democratic impulse.

APPENDICES

APPENDIX ONE

Quebec Figures

NOTE: For names and terms with an asterisk, see the entry in this or the following appendix.

HUBERT AQUIN (Montreal, 1929 – Montreal, 1977) Writer. Senior editor of the journal *Liberté** (1961–71). From 1960 a member of the Rassemblement pour l'Indépendence Nationale (RIN),* which he left, disaffected, in 1968. Arrested in 1964 for possession of a weapon, incarcerated, and later committed to the Albert Prévost psychiatric institution, where he wrote his first book, *Prochain épisode* (1965; translated as *Next Episode*,* 2001). Editor of Éditions La Presse (1975–76), which he left after a well-publicized disagreement with the daily's managing editor, Roger Lemelin. Also published *Trou de mémoire* (1968, winner of the Governor General's Literary Award, 1969, which he declined; translated as *Blackout*, 1974), *L'antiphonaire* (1969; translated as *The Antiphonary*, 1973), and *Neige noire* (1974; translated as *Hamlet's Twin*, 1979). Committed suicide in 1977.

Appendix One

PAUL-ÉMILE BORDUAS (Saint-Hilaire, 1905 – Paris, 1960)
Automatist* painter. Worked at Maurice Denis's Ateliers d'Art Sacré in Paris and was later influenced by surrealism and the work of Alfred Pellan. Professor at the École du Meuble de Montréal (1937–48). Co-founder of the Société d'Art Contemporain (1939). Co-author and signatory of the famous *Refus global** manifesto in 1948 (translated as *Total Refusal*, 1985). It was condemned by the authorities and cost him his position at the École du Meuble. In 1949, he published *Projections libérantes,* an autobiographical and educational work. Borduas went into exile, first in 1953 to New York and then in 1955 Paris, where he died in 1960.

HENRI BOURASSA (Montreal, 1868 – Outremont, 1952)
Journalist and politician. Proponent of a pan-Canadian nationalism whose main themes were relations between Canada and Britain, relations between Canada's French and English cultures, and the values that should guide economic life. Founder of the daily *Le Devoir** in 1910 and its editor-in-chief until 1932. Mayor of Montebello (1889–94) and Papineauville (1896–97). Member of the House of Commons for Labelle (1896–99, 1900–07, 1925–35). Ligue nationaliste member of the Quebec Legislative Assembly (1908–09).

MICHEL BRUNET (Montreal, 1917 – Montreal, 1985)
Historian. PhD from Clark University, Worcester, Mass. History professor at the Université de Montréal (1959–68). President of the Institut d'Histoire de l'Amérique Française (1970–71). Associated with the Montreal school of historical writing. His specific focus was on the consequences of the Conquest. Most notable among his works are *Canadians et*

Canadiens: Études sur l'histoire et la pensée des deux Canadas (1954), *La présence anglaise et les Canadiens* (1958), *Les Canadiens après la Conquète, 1759–1775* (Governor General's Literacy Award, 1969), and *Histoire politique, économique et sociale du Québec et des Québécois* (1975).

PAUL CHAMBERLAND (Longueuil, 1939 –)
Poet and essayist. Co-founder in 1963 of the journal *Parti pris*.* Studied literature and philosophy in Montreal and later in Paris, from where he returned marked by the events of May 1968. Published works of poetry include *Genèses* (1962), *Le pays* (1963, a collaborative work), *Terre Québec* (1964), *L'afficheur hurle* (1965), and *L'inavouable* (1968). Participated in the "Poetry Night" of 1970. During the 1970s, contributed to the magazines *Mainmise* and *Hobo-Québec*. Since 1992 a professor of literature at the Université du Québec à Montréal.

ANDRÉ D'ALLEMAGNE (Montreal, 1929 – Montreal, 2001)
Political scientist. Founder and first president of the RIN in 1960 and a member of the party's steering committee until it was dissolved in 1968. Defeated as RIN candidate in the Outremont riding in 1966. Holder of master's degrees in political science and linguistics. Began teaching political science in 1968 at CÉGEP de Maisonneuve. His books about Quebec include *Le colonialisme au Québec* (1966), *Le RIN et les débuts du mouvement indépendantiste québécois* (1974), and *Une idée qui somnolait: Écrits sur la souveraineté du Québec depuis les origines du RIN* (2000).

LÉON DION (Saint-Arsène, 1922 – Sillery, 1997)
Political scientist and sociologist. PhD in political science from the Université Laval; from 1954 on, a professor of political science there. During his career, Dion taught at

approximately thirty Canadian and American universities. Special adviser to the Royal Commission on Bilingualism and Biculturalism (1963–70) and the Canadian Unity Task Force (1977–79). Author of many books, including *Société et politique: La vie des groupes* (2 vols., 1971–72), *Quebec, the Unfinished Revolution* (1976), *À la recherche du Québec* (1987), *Les intellectuels et le temps de Duplessis* (1993), and *Le duel constitutionnel Canada-Québec* (1995).

FERNAND DUMONT (Montmorency, 1927 – Quebec, 1997)
Sociologist, theologian, philosopher, and poet. PhD in sociology and theology (Université Laval). Professor of sociology at Laval from 1955 to 1997. Produced a great deal of research on the theory of culture and the evolution of Quebec society. Published more than twenty books, including *Le lieu de l'homme* (1968), *Les idéologies* (1974), *Le sort de la culture* (1987), *Genèse de la société québécoise* (1993), and *Raisons communes* (1995), as well as several poetry collections. Co-founder of the Quebec studies journal *Recherches sociographiques*. Worked with the Ministère d'État au Développement Culturel (1977–78) on a cultural development policy for Quebec (White Paper, 1978). President and founder in 1979 of the Institut Québécois de Recherche sur la Culture, which he directed until 1990.

MAURICE LE NOBLET DUPLESSIS
(Trois-Rivières, 1890 – Schefferville, 1959)
Politician and lawyer. Premier of Quebec for eighteen years (1936–39 and 1944–59). Member of the Legislative Assembly for Trois-Rivières from 1927. Leader of the provincial Conservative Party in 1933. Founded the Union Nationale party in 1935, which brought together Conservative and Liberal dissidents. "Le Chef" led Quebec in a highly conservative

fashion, promising a form of nationalism based on the principle of provincial autonomy. He was known for his ruthless attitude towards "communists" (the "Padlock Law," 1937) and unions, and for his liberal economic policies. An agricultural credit program was established during his first mandate. Among his achievements during his second administration were the adoption of the Quebec flag (1948) and the implementation of a provincial income tax (1954). His legacy remains steeped in controversy.

GUY FRÉGAULT (Montreal, 1918 – Quebec, 1977)
Senior civil servant and historian associated with the Montreal school. PhD from Loyola University, Chicago. Director of the Institut d'Histoire de l'Amérique Française (1946–59) and chair of the history department of the University of Ottawa (1959–61). First holder of the position of Quebec deputy minister of cultural affairs (1961–66 and 1970–75). Author of numerous historical works, including *Iberville, le conquérant* (1944), *François Bigot, administrateur français* (1948), *La Guerre de Conquête* (1955; translated as *Canada: the War of the Conquest*, 1969), and *Le XVIIIe siècle canadien* (1968). Studied under Lionel Groulx* and later wrote a book about him, *Lionel Groulx tel qu'en lui-même*.

GÉRALD GODIN (Trois-Rivières, 1939 – Montreal, 1994)
Poet, journalist, and politician. Journalist from 1958 to 1963 with *Le Nouvelliste* and *Le Nouveau Journal*. Researcher and news editor at Radio-Canada (1963–69). Founding member of *Parti pris** and director of Éditions Parti Pris until 1976. Journalist at *Québec-Presse* (1969–74). Parti Québécois member of the National Assembly (1976–94), having been elected over Robert Bourassa in the Mercier riding. Minister of cultural communities and immigration, 1980–85, during

Appendix One

the René Lévesque and Pierre-Marc Johnson administrations. A retrospective collection of his poems, *Ils ne demandaient qu'à brûler*, was published in 1987.

LIONEL GROULX (Vaudreuil, 1878 – Vaudreuil, 1967) Priest, historian, and essayist. PhD in philosophy and theology from Minerva University, Rome (1907–08). History professor at the Université de Montréal from 1915 to 1949. Senior editor of *Action française* (1920–28) and contributor to numerous newspapers and journals, including *Le Devoir** and *L'Action nationale*. Founder of the Institut d'Histoire de l'Amérique Française in 1946 and *Revue d'histoire de l'Amérique française*, which he edited until his death. Author of numerous works, including the novel *L'appel de la race* (1922; translated as *The Iron Wedge*, 1986), *Notre maître le passé* (1924), *L'enseignement français au Canada* (1933), *Histoire du Canada français* (4 vols., 1950–52), *Notre grande aventure: L'empire français en Amérique* (1958), and *Chemins de l'avenir* (1964). Groulx, an inspiration to generations of historians and intellectuals, was given a state funeral.

JEAN HAMELIN (Saint-Narcisse, 1931 – Sainte-Foy, 1998)
Historian. PhD from the École Pratique des Hautes Études (Paris, 1957). Professor of history at Université Laval for thirty-six years. Published a large number of works, usually in collaboration with colleagues, on the economic and social history of Quebec and French Canada, including *Histoire économique du Québec*, 1851–1896 (in collaboration with Yves Roby; Governor General's Literary Award, 1972) and *Histoire du catholicisme québécois* (2 vols., in collaboration with Nicole Gagnon; Governor General's Award, 1985). Co-editor of the *Dictionary of Canadian Biography/Dictionnaire biographique du Canada* from 1973 to 1998.

Quebec Figures

ANDRÉ LAURENDEAU (Montreal, 1912 – Ottawa, 1968)
Journalist and author. Contributor (1934–37) and senior editor (1937–43, 1948–54) of the journal *L'Action nationale*. Bloc Populaire Canadien member of the Legislative Assembly (1944–48) and leader of the Quebec wing of the party. Editorialist, associate editor (1947–57), and senior editor (1957–68) of *Le Devoir*.* Radio-Canada television host (1952–61). Co-chair of the Royal Commission on Bilingualism and Biculturalism (Laurendeau-Dunton Commission, 1963–68). Kept a diary during the course of the commission's work (published 1990; translated as *The Diary of André Laurendeau*, 1991).

CAMILLE LAURIN (Charlemagne, 1922 – Outremont, 1999)
Psychiatrist and politician. Founding member of the Mouvement Souveraineté-Association (see "Sovereignty-Association"). Elected president of the Executive Committee of the Parti Québécois at its inception in 1968. PQ member of the Legislative Assembly (1970–73, 1976–84, 1994–98). Minister under René Lévesque's administration (1976–85). Father of the Charter of the French Language (Bill 101, 1977), which made French the only official language of Quebec. Resigned from his cabinet position in 1984 in protest over Lévesque's *"beau risque"* (the decision, after the 1980 referendum, to work towards constitutional reform rather than sovereignty, through negotiation with Brian Mulroney's government). With Jacques Parizeau at the head of the PQ, Laurin was re-elected in the Bourget riding in 1994. Director of the Hôpital Sacré-Cœur de Montréal from 1986 until his death.

ADÈLE LAUZON (Montreal, 1931 –)
Journalist. Associate member of the Confederation of Catholic Workers, the predecessor to the Confédération des Syndicats

Appendix One

Nationaux (CSN), one of the principal Quebec labour federations. Worked for the CSN's Federation of Needletrade, Industrial and Textile Workers. Contributed to *Vrai* and *Travail* (1956). Journalist with *La Presse** (1958–60). Wrote feature articles for *Maclean's* (1960–65). Researcher for the Radio-Canada television program *Femmes d'aujourd'hui* (1968–69) and the daily *Montreal Star* (1969–71). In charge of research for the Office of the Premier of Quebec (1978–80).

JEAN-MARC LÉGER (Montreal, 1927 –)
Journalist and senior civil servant. Co-initiator of the Francophonie, the multilateral organization of French-speaking nations. Journalist with *La Presse** (1951–57) and *Le Devoir** (1957–69). Secretary general and co-founder of the Association des Universités Partiellement et Entièrement de Langue Française (association of French-language universities; 1961–78). First president of the Office de la Langue Française (1962–63). Secretary general of the Agence de Coopération Culturelle et Technique des Pays de Langue Française (1969–74). Quebec delegate general in Brussels (1978–81). Assistant deputy minister of education (1981–84). Assistant deputy minister of international relations (1984–89). Director of the Fondation Lionel-Groulx (1989–98). Published, among other works, *La Francophonie: Grand dessein, grande ambiguïté* (1987) and *Vers l'indépendance?* (1993).

PIERRE MAHEU (Montreal, 1939 – Montreal, 1979)
Essayist. Co-founder in 1963 and principal editor of the journal *Parti pris*.* Also a filmmaker with the National Film Board and a publicist for both the Mouvement Souveraineté-Association and the PQ. Author of *Un Parti pris révolutionnaire* (1983).

Quebec Figures

GILLES MARCOTTE (Sherbrooke, 1925 –)
Professor, writer, and literary critic. Journalist with *Le Devoir** (1948–55) and *La Presse** (1961–66). PhD in French literature (Université Laval). Professor of literature at the Université de Montréal from 1966. Author of several books, including novels (*Le poids de Dieu*, 1962; translated as *The Burden of God*, 1964; *Retour à Coolbrook*, 1965; *Une mission difficile*, 1977), stories (*La mort de Duplessis et autres récits*, 1999), and essays (*Une littérature qui se fait*, 1962; *Le temps des poètes*, 1969; *Le roman à l'imparfait*, 1976; *La prose de Rimbaud*, 1984).

GASTON MIRON (Sainte-Agathe-des-Monts, 1928 – Montreal, 1996)
Poet and editor. Considered by many to be Quebec's national poet. Co-founder of Éditions de l'Hexagone (1953) and its principal editor until 1983. Helped to found the magazine *Liberté** in 1959. Member from 1963 to 1968 of the *Parti pris** team. *L'homme rapaillé* (1970; selections translated as *The Agonized Life: Poems and Prose*, 1980; also translated in several other languages) is a collection of his poems published in various newspapers and journals. Won numerous awards and honours in Canada and abroad, including the Prix Apollinaire (Paris, 1981) and the Molson Prize from the Canada Council for the Arts (1985), as well as the title of *commandeur des arts et des lettres* of France (honorary badge; 1993). First Quebec writer to be honoured with a state funeral.

FERNAND OUELLET (Lac-Bouchette, 1926 –)
Historian. PhD from Université Laval. Professor emeritus at York University. Holder of the Robarts Chair in Canadian Studies (1985–86). Author of various works on Quebec and French Canada, including *Histoire economique et sociale du*

Québec, 1760–1850 (1966; translated as *Economic and Social History of Quebec, 1760–1850*, 1980) and *Le Bas-Canada, 1791–1840: Changements structuraux et crise* (1976; translated as *Lower Canada, 1791–1840*, 1980). Ouellet broke with the nationalist historiographic tradition, favouring quantitative methods and the study of social classes.

GÉRARD PELLETIER (Victoriaville, 1919 – Victoriaville, 1997)
Journalist, politician, diplomat, and essayist. Journalist at *Le Devoir** (1947–50). Co-founder in 1950 of *Cité libre.** Senior editor of *La Presse** (1961–65). Member of Parliament from 1965 to 1975. Headed several departments during the Pearson and Trudeau administrations, including Communications from 1972 to 1975. Canadian ambassador to Paris (1975–81) and to the United Nations (1981–85). Published his memoirs in three volumes: *Les années d'impatience* (1983; translated as *Years of Impatience, 1950–1960*, 1984), *Le temps des choix* (1985; translated as *Years of Choice, 1960–1968*, 1987), and *L'aventure du pouvoir* (1992).

MARCEL RIOUX (Amqui, 1919 – Amqui, 1992)
Sociologist. Undergraduate degree in political and social science from the Université de Paris. Professor of sociology at the Université de Montréal from 1961. Research focused on the Iroquois, rural and urban communities, and Quebec youth. Between 1966 and 1968 chaired Quebec's royal commission on arts education (Commission d'enquête sur l'enseignement des arts au Québec). Contributed to the work of the Royal Commission on Bilingualism and Biculturalism. His works include *La question du Québec* (1969; translated as *Quebec in Question*, 1971), *Deux pays pour vivre* (1980), and *Un peuple dans le siècle* (1990).

Quebec Figures

PAUL SAUVÉ (Saint-Benoît, 1907 – Saint-Eustache, 1960)
Politician and lawyer. Elected to the Legislative Assembly on the Conservative Party ticket in a by-election in 1930. Defeated in 1935, then re-elected under the Union Nationale banner in 1936. Minister in the Duplessis cabinet from 1946 to 1959. Succeeded Duplessis as premier on 11 September 1959. Announced a political renewal and major reforms, but died in office on 2 January 1960.

MAURICE SÉGUIN (Horse Creek, Sask., 1918 – Lorraine, Que., 1984)
Associated with the Montreal school* of historians. PhD from the Université de Montréal. Became a history professor there and succeeded Guy Frégault* in the Lionel-Groulx Chair (1959–84). A theorist of neo-nationalism* and the contemporary Quebec separatist movement (1959–84), Séguin was the guiding light of a whole generation of historians. His theoretical work on the nature of international relations, based on the relationship between "the two Canadas" since 1760, led to an influential set of lectures known as *Les normes*. His works include *La Conquête et la vie économique des Canadiens* (1946) and *L'idée d'indépendance au Québec* (1967).

MARCEL TRUDEL (Saint-Narcisse, 1917 -)
Historian. PhD from Université Laval, 1945. Professor of history there from 1947, then at Carleton University, and finally at the University of Ottawa from 1966 to 1982. Co-editor of the *Dictionary of Canadian Biography/Dictionnaire biographique du Canada*. Author of numerous books, including several on the beginnings of New France: *L'influence de Voltaire au Canada* (1945), *L'esclavage au Canada français* (1960), *Initiation*

à la Nouvelle-France (1968; translated as *Introduction to New France*, 1976), and *Mythes et réalités de l'histoire du Québec* (1963). President of the Canadian Historical Association (1963–64) and the Institut d'Histoire de l'Amérique Française (1972–73).

PIERRE VADEBONCŒUR (Montreal, 1920 –)
Essayist. Adviser to the Confédération des Syndicats Nationaux from 1950 to 1975, he was intimately involved in workers' struggles for socialism and Quebec independence. His political and polemical essays, as well as the many articles he published in newspapers and journals since 1940 (in *Cité libre*,* *Parti pris*,* *Liberté*,* *Le Devoir*,* etc.), testify to his commitment. His works include *La ligne du risque* (1963), *Un génocide en douce* (1976), *Les deux royaumes* (1978), and *Vivement un autre siècle* (1996).

PIERRE VALLIÈRES (Montreal, 1938 – Montreal, 1998)
Journalist, author, and activist. Contributor to *Le Devoir** (1957–62) and *La Presse** (1963–65). After serving as senior editor of *Cité libre** for a few months (1963–64), he left to found *Révolution québécoise* (1964–65) along with Charles Gagnon. Also instrumental in the founding of *Parti pris*.* Joined the Front de Libération du Québec (FLQ) in 1965. Demonstrated in support of the FLQ in New York in 1966; arrested and deported to Canada in 1967; convicted but later acquitted. In prison he wrote *Nègres blancs d'Amérique* (1968; translated as *White Niggers of America*,* 1971). Also published *L'éxécution de Pierre Laporte* (1977; translated as *The Assassination of Pierre Laporte*, 1977), *La démocratie ingouvernable* (1979), *La liberté en friche* (1979), and *Le devoir de la résistance* (1994).

APPENDIX TWO

Quebec Institutions, Events, and Concepts

NOTE: For names and terms with an asterisk, see the entry in this or the preceding appendix.

ALLOPHONE   A person whose mother tongue is a foreign language in the country or community in which he or she lives. In Quebec the term refers to people whose mother tongue is neither French nor English.

ARGUMENT   Semi-annual journal founded in Quebec City in 1998 and edited by the philosopher Daniel Jacques. *Argument* seeks to be a forum for the discussion of issues of concern to contemporary Quebec society. The articles and features cover social and political questions as well as a variety of other themes, such as rock music, technological utopias, and Native politics. The honorary editorial committee is comprised of Lise Bissonnette (former senior editor of *Le Devoir**), French philosopher Alain Finkielkraut, and Professors Guy Laforest and Charles Taylor.

AUTOMATISM   An art movement in Quebec whose name is derived from the title of a painting by Paul-Émile Borduas.* The term also refers to a technique used by surrealist writers (André Breton's automatic writing). The movement developed in Montreal between 1941 and 1954 in reaction to the prevailing academicist approach to the fine arts. Besides Borduas, the automatists included Fernand Leduc, Jean-Paul Riopelle, Marcel Barbeau, Marcelle Ferron, and Pierre Gauvreau. The group's first exhibitions were held in Montreal and Paris in 1946 and 1947. Their manifesto, known as *Refus global*,* led the automatists onto political terrain, but the group broke up soon after its publication.

CITÉ LIBRE   Journal founded in 1950 by Gérard Pelletier* and Pierre Elliott Trudeau (first series, 1950–59; second series, 1960–66). Secular, critical of the clergy and of nationalism, humanist, progressive, the journal brought together intellectuals opposed to Premier Maurice Duplessis* who were inspired by liberal thinkers and the personalism of Emmanuel Mounier. During the 1950s *Cité libre* was one of the main forums of opposition to the established order and a harbinger of the Quiet Revolution.* Differences between the federalist and separatist contributors led the latter to quit the journal, which was replaced by *Cahiers de Cité libre* in 1966. A third series began in 1991 under the direction of Gérard Pelletier's daughter, Anne-Marie Bourdouxhe. This time, the journal was revived in order to champion viewpoints critical of "nationalist unanimity," and regular meetings were held with its readership. In 1995 Monique and Max Nemni took over editorial duties, and the journal soon became "the Quebec voice of liberalism and Canadian unity." An English version was launched in 1998. *Cité libre* ceased publishing in the summer of 2000.

COMMISSION ON THE POLITICAL AND CONSTITUTIONAL FUTURE OF QUEBEC (BÉLANGER-CAMPEAU COMMISSION)   Commission created in 1990 under the authority of the

Quebec Institutions, Events, and Concepts

National Assembly* following the failure of the Meech Lake agreement. The commission's mandate was to study and analyze Quebec's political and constitutional status. Co-chaired by Michel Bélanger and Jean Campeau, it heard from representatives of the Quebec government, the official opposition, and various interest groups. The commission's report, tabled in 1991, recommended the enactment of a bill mandating a referendum on Quebec sovereignty.

LE DEVOIR Montreal daily founded in 1910 by Henri Bourassa.* An independent nationalist newspaper originally dedicated to the protection of Catholic values and the advocacy of French-Canadian rights, as well as the promotion of Canadian independence from Britain. It opposed conscription in 1917 and 1942; it also opposed the Duplessis* government during its second mandate. In 1976 *Le Devoir*'s senior editor, a federalist, wrote an editorial backing the Parti Québécois in the election. During the 1980 referendum on sovereignty-association,* the acting senior editor came out in support of the No vote, but three members of the editorial staff supported the Yes side. During the 1995 referendum, it was the only paper in Quebec to back the Yes option. Senior editors since 1963: Claude Ryan (1963–77), Michel Roy (acting, 1978–81), Jean-Claude Roy (1981–96), Benoît Lauzière (1986–90), Lise Bissonnette (1990–98), and Bernard Descôteaux (since 1998).

GREAT DARKNESS A term referring to the period from the 1930s to the Quiet Revolution,* in which the dominant figure was Premier Maurice Duplessis.* If the Quiet Revolution symbolizes openness to modernity, the Great Darkness evokes a climate in which the power of the church and other forces stifled intellectuals and progressive elements in

Appendix Two

Quebec society. However, some historians believe a more nuanced view is in order, arguing that signs of modernity in Quebec were already evident during this period.

LIBERTÉ   Bimonthly journal founded in 1959 in Montreal by the poet Jean-Guy Pilon and several other writers. A prestigious and politically involved literary magazine open to all literary genres. Published now-famous texts, including Gaston Miron's* poem cycle *La vie agonique*, Hubert Aquin's* "La fatigue culturelle du Canada-français," and the early writings of future *Parti pris** members. Also welcomed the work of foreign writers such as René Char, Aimé Césaire, Milan Kundera, Julio Cortazar, and René Girard. Since its founding, edited successively by Jean-Guy Pilon, Jacques Godbout, Hubert Aquin, François Ricard, François Hébert, and Marie-Andrée Lamontagne.

MONTREAL SCHOOL   A school of historical interpretation whose principal representatives were Guy Frégault,* Maurice Séguin,* and Michel Brunet.* This school, which developed during the 1950s, has influenced two generations of historians. It sought to break from the paradigm of *survivance** characteristic of traditional historical approaches, while remaining loyal to nationalism (see neo-nationalism*).

NATIONAL ASSEMBLY   Name of the Quebec legislative assembly since 1968. It refers to both the members of the assembly and the place where they sit. Under the British North America Act of 1867, the Quebec assembly was comprised of a lieutenant-governor, a Legislative Council appointed by the lieutenant-governor, and a Legislative Assembly elected by the population. The Legislative Council was abolished in 1968, and the Legislative Assembly was renamed the National Assembly. This body exercises legislative power in conjunction with the lieutenant-governor.

NEO-NATIONALISM   Reformist version of nationalism developing in the 1950s, whose aim was to adapt French-Canadian nationalism to the post-war reality of Quebec. Its principal originators were Guy Frégault,* Maurice Séguin*, and Michel Brunet* of the Montreal school.* While maintaining the objective of asserting the national identity of the French-Canadian people, neo-nationalism seeks to replace the traditionalist aspects of this doctrine (*survivance**) with values better suited to an urban, industrial, contemporary Quebec. It also advocates an independent Quebec state as a means of affirming and defending the nation. This movement was an important ideological source for the Quiet Revolution.

NEXT EPISODE   First novel by Hubert Aquin* originally published as *Prochain episode* (1965). A fragmented account of a neurotic haunted by suicide who, having become a terrorist and fallen in love, organizes a revolution with a group of FLQ patriots. He receives an order to go to Switzerland to kill an agent of the Canadian federalist forces. Following his failure, he is thrown in prison and transferred to a psychiatric clinic while awaiting trial. He relives his past, trying to understand what went wrong by imagining a spy novel. For many, *Next Episode*'s protagonist symbolizes the history of the Québécois people. English translations by Penny Williams (1967) and Sheila Fischman (2001).

PARTI PRIS   Political and cultural journal (1963–68), with an affiliated publishing house, founded by a group of young leftist writers and intellectuals. The first editorial board included André Major, Paul Chamberland,* Pierre Maheu,*

Appendix Two

Jean-Marc Piotte, and André Brochu. *Parti pris* promoted a revolution that would establish Quebec as an independent socialist and secular state. Marxist-Leninism, Sartrean existentialism, and the issues of decolonization were at the heart of its ideology. On the literary front, the journal had ties to the *joual* (dialect) literary movement that symbolized Québécois alienation. Les Éditions Parti pris published some important works such as *Nègres blancs d'Amériques* (*White Niggers of America**) by Pierre Vallières,* *L'afficheur hurle* by Paul Chamberland, and *Le cassé* by Jacques Renaud.

LA PRESSE   Montreal daily founded in 1884 by William-Edmond Blumhart and disaffected Conservatives from John A. Macdonald's government. Under the editorial hand of Trefflé Berthiaume (1899–1915), *La Presse* became a daily newspaper. Despite its original political orientation, many of the paper's editors and writers have been known for their liberal sympathies, especially since the 1950s. Paul Desmarais and the Gesca Group acquired ownership in 1967. Editors since the late 1950s: Jean-Louis Gagnon (1958–61), Gérard Pelletier* (1961–65), Roger Champoux (1965–69), Jean-Paul Desbiens (1969–72), Roger Lemelin (1972–80), Roger D. Landry (1980–2000), and Guy Crevier (since 2000). In 2000 the circulation fluctuated around 220,000 copies on weekdays and 320,000 on Saturdays, making it one of Quebec's largest-circulation publications.

QUIET REVOLUTION   A term referring to the changes that took place in Quebec from 1960 on, coined by a *Globe and Mail* journalist. In its strictest sense, it refers to the period from 1960 to 1966, when the principal reforms of Jean Lesage's Liberal government were implemented. At this time, most of the education, health, and social responsibilities previously held by the Catholic Church were transferred to the government. However, in a more general sense, the term refers to the 1960s and 1970s, when the dominant themes were the welfare state and neo-nationalism.* The French term *affirmationisme* (translated in this book by its cognate) is also used to describe this general movement.

RASSEMBLEMENT POUR L'INDÉPENDANCE NATIONALE (RIN)   Movement founded in 1960 to promote Quebec independence; became a political party in 1963. In the 1966 elections the RIN garnered close to 6 per cent of the vote, but none of its candidates were elected. The arrival of the Mouvement Souveraineté-Association on the scene in 1967 provoked a crisis within the party, and it folded in 1968 with the founding of the Parti Québécois. Most of the RIN's 14,000 members joined the PQ.

REFUS GLOBAL   Manifesto published in 1948 whose principal essay was written by Paul-Émile Borduas* and endorsed by fifteen members of the automatist* movement. It called for a liberation of aesthetics from academicism, questioned traditional values (the Catholic faith and attachment to ancestral values), and championed an ideal of greater artistic and intellectual freedom. These ideas scandalized the authorities, costing Borduas his position at the École du Meuble. In the months that followed, approximately one hundred articles condemning the manifesto were printed in various newspapers and magazines. Nevertheless, the text and its authors had a huge impact on the Quebec art world.

SOVEREIGNTY-ASSOCIATION   A form of political autonomy in which certain powers and institutions, especially economic ones, are shared among several states. The term appeared for

Appendix Two

the first time in René Lévesque's book *Option Québec* (1968). It described the main objective of the Mouvement Souveraineté-Association and later the Parti Québécois: political independence for Quebec, together with an economic association with the rest of Canada, which would include a free-trade zone and a common monetary system. In the 1980 referendum the Quebec government asked Quebecers for a mandate to negotiate for sovereignty-association with the federal government and the other provinces. The proposal was rejected by 60 per cent of the voters. In 1985 the PQ removed this option from its electoral platform. The "sovereignty partnership" formula voted on in the 1995 referendum is closely related to sovereignty-association.

SUPREME COURT DECISION IN THE REFERENCE ON QUEBEC SECESSION (1998)   Decision regarding the constitutionality of the possible secession of Quebec. In the Supreme Court of Canada's opinion, a unilateral declaration of independence is unconstitutional from the standpoint of both constitutional and international law; however, Quebec could hold a referendum on secession, and with a "clear majority" in favour on a "clear question," the rest of Canada would be constitutionally obligated to negotiate the terms of Quebec's independence. The Court left it up to the political actors to determine what should be considered a "clear question" and a "clear majority." In June 2000 the Canadian Parliament passed Bill C-20 (known as the "Clarity Act"), claiming that it had thereby complied with the clarity requirement laid down by the Court.

SUPREME COURT DECISION OF 1988 *(FORD VS. P.G. QUÉBEC)* In this December 1988 judgment, also known as the Ford decision, the Supreme Court of Canada ruled that sections 58 (public signs and posters) and 69 (company names) of the

Charter of the French Language (Bill 101) violated section 3 of the Quebec Charter of Human Rights and Freedoms. The Court concluded that the prohibition of all languages other than French in public signs and posters and in commercial advertising infringes freedom of expression. However, it did recognize the legitimacy of a "clear predominance" of French, so as to promote and preserve the French "linguistic landscape" of Quebec.

SURVIVANCE   The dominant self-representation of francophone Quebecers before the 1960s – literally, "survival." The word was originally applied to affirmative struggles to preserve French culture and language; for example, the "Flint Affair," in which French Canadians living in a New England sawmill town engaged in various acts of religious disobedience to force the Catholic authorities to appoint a French-speaking pastor. However, commentators since the Montreal school* have increasingly used the word in a more pejorative sense to refer to a syndrome in which the francophone culture cannot achieve its full potential, essentially because it has become historically conditioned to think in terms of threats to its survival. As a result, survivance has come to connote subsistence, "surviving in lieu of thriving."

WHITE NIGGERS OF AMERICA   Autobiographical essay by Pierre Vallières* published as Nègres blancs d'Amérique in 1968 (English translation, 1971, by Joan Pinkham). The author recounts his coming to revolutionary awareness, presenting a Marxist analysis of Quebec and a revolutionary agenda. According to Vallières, the Quebec working class has the characteristics of a colonized people, hence the term "white niggers." He believed that only through armed revolution could the situation be changed.

Notes

PREFACE

1 Michel Venne, "Un pont entre deux rives: Entrevue avec Graham Fraser," *Le Devoir*, 19 May 2001, D4.
2 See Quebec, *Vision: A Policy Statement on Immigration and Integration* (Montréal: Ministère des communautés culturelles et de l'immigration, 1990); and Joseph H. Carens, *Culture, Citizenship, and Community* (Oxford: Oxford University Press, 2000), 107–39.
3 In another context but during the same period, Michaud also said that the Jewish people were not the only ones who had suffered throughout history.
4 See chapter 4 for a more detailed account.
5 Quebec, *Vision: A Policy Statement*, 15.
6 Alain-G. Gagnon, "Plaidoyer pour l'interculturalisme," *Possibles* 24, no. 4 (2000): 11–25.

INTRODUCTION

1 Political philosophy's fascination with multiculturalism often leads to the hybridity of contemporary societies' being overlooked. Although the concept of multiculturalism is essential

to understanding the peaceful coexistence of different and somewhat mutually exclusive cultural groups (one thinks of the relations between Montreal's Hasidic community and its neighbours), it can easily ignore mixing, overlap, interpenetration, and cross-pollination between cultural communities. As Sherry Simon posits, "multiculturalism conceives of cultures as autonomous totalities. Each 'we' of multiculturalism designates an easily identifiable and separable group defined by its beliefs, customs, and habits" (Simon, *Hybridité culturelle* [Montréal: L'île de la tortue, 1999], 19).

2 Following a series of debates on the Quebec nation organized by the newspaper *Le Devoir* in conjunction with McGill University's Quebec Studies Program, the editorialist Michel Venne concluded that "the national question is one that still raises tremendous interest, in spite of all the nonsense written about constitutional fatigue. We have a desire and a need to debate the collective future of Quebecers, and it is greater than the monotony of the media leads one to believe. As soon as one backs off from the quarrelling of politicians and gets back to the root of things, the topic comes up again" (Venne, "La nation québécoise," *Le Devoir*, 18–19 September 1999, A10). Revised and expanded versions of these essays were collected in *Vive Quebec! New Thinking and New Approaches to the Quebec Nation*, ed. M. Venne, trans. Robert Chodos and Louisa Blair (Toronto: James Lorimer, 2001).

3 Concerning the effects of the Charter, the interpretation of Alan Cairns, a political science professor at the University of British Columbia, is relevant: "The Charter is not playing around with the externals of our existence. Over time, the cumulative results of its application will reach deeply into our innermost being, manipulating our psyche and transforming our self-image" (Cairns, *Disruptions: Constitutional Struggles, from the Charter to Meech Lake*, ed. D.E. Williams [Toronto: McClelland & Stewart, 1991], 62).

Notes to pages 6–9

4 Guy Laforest, *Trudeau and the End of a Canadian Dream,* trans. Paul Leduc Browne and Michelle Weinroth (Montreal: McGill-Queen's University Press, 1995). On the different visions of federalism put forward by Quebec and the rest of Canada, see Will Kymlicka, "Multinational Federalism in Canada: Rethinking the Partnership," in *Beyond the Impasse: Toward Reconciliation,* ed. G. Laforest and Roger Gibbins (Montreal: Institute for Research on Public Policy, 1998).
5 See James Tully, "Introduction," in *Multinational Democracies,* ed. Alain-G. Gagnon and J. Tully (Cambridge: Cambridge University Press, 2001), 1–33.
6 Charles Taylor, "The Stakes of Constitutional Reform," in *Reconciling the Solitudes: Essays on Federalism and Nationalism,* ed. Guy Laforest, trans. Ruth Abbey for this essay (Montreal: McGill-Queen's University Press, 1993), 141, 145.
7 Jocelyn Maclure, "Identité et politique: Penser la nation politique à l'ère des identités multiples," *Possibles* 24 (spring–summer 2000): 229–39.
8 See James Tully, *The Unattained yet Attainable Democracy: Canada and Quebec Face the New Century: The Desjardins Lecture* (Montreal: Quebec Studies Program, McGill University, 2000)
9 For an exemplification of the "sovereigntist by default" position, see Alain-G. Gagnon and François Rocher, "Faire l'histoire au lieu de la subir," in *Répliques aux détracteurs de la souveraineté,* ed. A.-G. Gagnon and F. Rocher (Montréal: VLB, 1992), 27–47.
10 For an analysis that takes account of factors both endogenous and exogenous to Quebec society, see Jocelyn Létourneau, *Les années sans guide: Le Canada à l'ère de l'économie migrante* (Montréal: Boréal, 1996).
11 Martin Heidegger, *Being and Time,* trans. Joan Stambaugh (Albany: State University of New York Press, 1996).
12 Zygmunt Bauman, "From Pilgrim to Tourist – or a Short History of Identity," in *Questions of Cultural Identity,* ed.

Stuart Hall (London: Sage, 1996), 18–36; Charles Taylor, "The Politics of Recognition," in *Multiculturalism and "The Politics of Recognition,"* ed. Amy Gutmann (Princeton: Princeton University Press, 1992).

13 Mikhaël Elbaz, "Introduction," in *Les frontières de l'identité: Modernité et postmodernisme au Québec*, ed. M. Elbaz, Andrée Fortin, and Guy Laforest (Sainte-Foy: Presses de l'Université Laval, 1996), 8.

14 For Dumont, fundamental values such as truth and democracy necessitate this interpretive work: "At bottom, the utopia of a body of knowledge that would rally the unanimous adherence of its compilers, and the utopia of a polity that would give rise to a convergence of freedoms, both presuppose an even more distant utopia: a community of those who interpret history" (Fernand Dumont, *Récit d'une émigration: Mémoires* [Montréal: Boréal, 1997], 296).

15 In writings about the "end of the nation," one often finds the argument that the nation has been deserted as a site of identity by young people, for whom the virtual has become reality. But as Jocelyn Létourneau contends, "it is the nation – given its reality already (often) institutionalized in the form of the state, its international recognition, its effective history, its materiality, and its functional unity – which remains for young people the primary referent in relation to which we situate and express ourselves, and from which we project ourselves into the world" (Létourneau, "La nation des jeunes," in *Les jeunes à l'ère de la mondialisation: Quête identitaire et conscience historique*, ed. Bogumil Jewsiewicki and J. Létourneau [Quebec: Septentrion, 1998], 412).

16 Fernand Dumont, *Genèse de la société québécoise* (Montréal: Boréal, 1993), 12.

17 Michel Seymour, *La nation en question* (Montréal: L'Hexagone, 1999), 98.

18 See Michel Foucault and Gilles Deleuze, "Intellectuals and Power," in *Language, Counter-Memory, Practice: Selected Essays and Interviews*, ed. Donald F. Bouchard, trans. D.F. Bouchard and Sherry Simon for this essay (Ithaca, NY: Cornell University Press, 1977), 205–17.
19 See David Owen, "Orientation and Enlightenment: An Essay on Genealogy and Critique," in *Foucault contra Habermas*, ed. Samantha Ashenden and D. Owen (London: Sage, 1999).
20 Michel Foucault, "The Masked Philosopher," in *Ethics: Subjectivity and Truth*, trans. Alan Sheridan for this essay (New York: New Press, 1997), 327. The reader will rapidly realize that Foucault's late work constitutes the backdrop to my theoretical approach. Ludwig Wittgenstein's work also leads us in this direction; he writes that "philosophy is a battle against the bewitchment of our intelligence by means of language" (Wittgenstein, *Philosophical Investigations*, trans. G. E. M. Anscombe [Oxford: Basil Blackwell, 1967], 47, par. 109).
21 As Gérard Bouchard points out, representations of the self and the other are central to the concept of the social imaginary: "The imaginary is therefore the product of the set of processes or procedures whereby a society adopts bearings in space and time, in order to make communication possible among its members and to situate itself with respect to other societies" (Bouchard, *L'histoire comparée des collectivités neuves: Une autre perspective pour les études québécoises: Les grandes conférences Desjardins* [Montreal: Quebec Studies Program, McGill University, 1999], 4).
22 On this subject, see the interesting column by Pierre Foglia, "Une soirée culturelle," *La Presse*, 7 October 1999, A5.
23 Alain Dubuc, "Tourner la page," *La Presse*, 19 February 2000. It is perhaps worth stressing that Dubuc's columns also contain ideas that can help to move the debate forward.

24 Jean-François Lisée, *Sortie de secours: Comment échapper au déclin du Québec* (Montréal: Boréal, 2000), 19–64.
25 In doing so, I will draw rather freely on the Cambridge contextualist school, of which Quentin Skinner is undoubtedly one of the foremost representatives. For a discussion of his work, see James Tully, ed., *Meaning and Context: Quentin Skinner and His Critics* (Princeton: Princeton University Press, 1988).
26 Michel Foucault, "What Is Enlightenment?" in *Ethics: Subjectivity and Truth*, trans. Catherine Porter for this essay (New York: New Press, 1997), 316.
27 Michel Foucault, "Polemics, Politics and Problematizations," in *Ethics: Subjectivity and Truth*, trans. Lydia Davis for this essay, 112.
28 James Tully, "Democracy and Globalization: A Defeasible Sketch," in *Canadian Political Philosophy: Contemporary Reflections*, ed. Ronald Beiner and Wayne Norman (Don Mills, Ont.: Oxford University Press, 2001). Wittgenstein's *Philosophical Investigations* are the best exemplification of this philosophical approach.
29 For a more detailed discussion of these issues, see Daniel Tanguay, "Requiem pour un conflit générationnel," *Argument* 1 (fall 1998): 58–80; and Éric Bédard's reply, "L'esprit-boomer n'a pas d'âge," *Argument* 2 (winter 2000): 142–9.

CHAPTER ONE

1 Sigmund Freud, "Mourning and Melancholia," in *The Freud Reader*, ed. Peter Gay (New York and London: W.W. Norton, 1989), 584.
2 "This melancholia constitutes one of the fundamental templates – and perhaps even the episteme in terms of memory and history – of past and contemporary Quebec literary and

scientific production" (Jocelyn Létourneau, "'Impenser' le pays et toujours l'aimer," *Cahiers internationaux de sociologie* 105 [1998]: 363; see also, by the same author, "Pour une révolution de la mémoire collective: Histoire et conscience historique chez les Québécois," *Argument* 1 [fall 1998]: 41–57). Jean Larose, whom I include here in my analysis of the melancholy social discourse, considers the Québécois to have never fully consoled themselves for the loss of the continent and, because of that, to be living in a state of perpetual "continental melancholy" (Larose, *L'amour du pauvre* [Montréal: Boréal, 1991], 87). See also philosopher Daniel Jacques's discussion of the "traumatic historical memory" of certain Quebec authors in his essay "La mort annoncée d'un projet insignifiant?" in *Possibles* 19 (winter-spring 1995): 216.

3 With the rise of the Parti Québécois and the separatist movement, the old identity descriptor "French Canadian" fell into disuse; nowadays, the vast majority of French-speaking Quebecers would refer to themselves as "Québécois."

4 Gérard Bouchard, *L'histoire comparée des collectivités neuves: Une autre perspective pour les études québécoises* (Montreal: Quebec Studies Program, McGill University, 1999), 26.

5 As I discuss below, the nationalist authors studied provide examples of historical, rather than metaphysical, essentialism. I have attempted a critique of substantialist interpretations of identity in Quebec in "Authenticités québécoises: Le Québec et la fragmentation contemporaine de l'identité," *Globe: Revue internationale d'études québécoises* 1 (November 1998): 9–35.

6 Paul-Émile Borduas, *Écrits/Writings* 1942–1958 (Halifax and New York: Nova Scotia College of Art and Design and New York University Press, 1978), 45.

7 Ronald Rudin, *Making History in Twentieth-Century Quebec* (Toronto: University of Toronto Press, 1997), 93.

8 Maurice Séguin, *Une histoire du Québec: Vision d'un prophète,* ed. Denis Vaugeois (Montréal: Guérin, 1995), 15.
9 As Jean Lamarre summarizes, "for neo-nationalism, a school of thought developed and epitomized by the Montreal historiographic school, the economic inferiority of the French Canadians, the retrograde nature of their institutions, the disproportionate influence of the clergy over the society, as well as the national phenomenon of *survivance,* are simply the various consequences of how the French Canadian historical process was severed by the English conquest" (Lamarre, *Le devenir de la nation québécoise selon Maurice Séguin, Guy Frégault et Michel Brunet (1944–1969)* [Sillery, Que.: Septentrion, 1993], 19).
10 Guy Frégault, *La guerre de la Conquête* (Montréal: Fides, 1954), 100.
11 Rudin, *Making History,* 129.
12 Denis Vaugeois considers Séguin, for example, as "perhaps the intellectual who has had the greatest influence on Quebec's progress since 1960" (Séguin, *Une histoire du Québec,* v). In more measured terms, people such as Jean Lamarre and Léon Dion consider the work of the Montreal historians to be of great importance in fashioning a modern Quebec nationalism; see Rudin, *Making History,* 96.
13 Séguin, *Une histoire du Québec,* 210.
14 Pierre Elliott Trudeau, "New Treason of the Intellectuals," in *Against the Current: Selected Writings, 1939–1966,* ed. Gérard Pelletier, new trans. George Tombs (Toronto: McClelland & Stewart, 1996).
15 Hubert Aquin, *Writing Quebec* (Edmonton: University of Alberta Press, 1988), 35.
16 Ibid., 42.
17 According to André-J. Bélanger, this kind of semantic shift is common currency in the writings of the *Parti pris* contributors,

Notes to pages 27–30

such as Paul Chamberland and Pierre Maheu (Bélanger, *Quatre idéologies du Québec en éclatement: La Relève, La* JEC, *Cité libre, Parti pris* [Montréal: Hurtubise HMH, 1977]). In fact, it is frequently found in the writings of the melancholy intellectuals in general. Jean Bouthillette, reflecting on his essay *Le Canadien français et son double* (Montréal: L'Hexagone, 1972), which is perhaps just as representative as the writings discussed here at greater length, admits that he "dared to make of [his] autobiography the biography of an entire people" (Bouthillette and Serge Cantin, "Lettres sur le Québec," *Liberté* 40 [December 1998]: 26).

18 Aquin, *Writing Quebec*, 42.
19 Hubert Aquin, *Next Episode* (Toronto: McClelland & Stewart 2001, trans. Sheila Fischman), 13–14. In a similar vein, the narrator in Aquin's novel *Blackout* (Toronto: House of Anansi, 1974, trans. Alan Brown) sighs, "Dear lost country, how like you I am" (95).
20 Aquin, *Writing Quebec*, 34.
21 Aquin, *Next Episode*, 98.
22 "Today I tend to think that our cultural existence can be something other than a perpetual challenge, and that the fatigue can come to an end" (Aquin, *Writing Quebec*, 42).
23 Aquin, *Blackout*, 27.
24 Gaston Miron, "A Lesson in Commitment," in *Embers and Earth (Selected Poems)*, trans. Marc Plourde for this essay (Montreal: Guernica Editions, 1984), 47. See also "October" in the same collection.
25 Gaston Miron, "Le bilingue de naissance," in *L'homme rapaillé* (Montréal: Typo, 1998), 221.
26 Miron, "A Long Road," in *Embers and Earth* (trans. Marc Plourde for this essay), 105, 112.
27 Bélanger, *Quatre idéologies*, 145. My reading of the *Parti pris* project draws heavily on Bélanger's interpretation.

28 Ibid., 147.
29 Ibid., 146.
30 Frantz Fanon, *The Wretched of the Earth*, trans. Constance Farrington (New York: Grove Press, 1968), 226.
31 The influence of thinkers such as Albert Memmi and Frantz Fanon on the *Parti pris* members and other anti-colonialist intellectuals has been repeatedly emphasized, so there is no need for me to belabour the point. See Fanon, *The Wretched of the Earth*, and A. Memmi, *The Colonizer and the Colonized*, trans. Howard Greenfeld (Boston: Beacon Press, 1991), as well as the important prefaces to these two works by Jean-Paul Sartre.
32 "As such, violence aimed either at overthrowing the state or mobilizing the populace was never rejected by the journal. If in general it did not contemplate violence, it was because it considered it unadvisable from a tactical standpoint" (Bélanger, *Quatre idéologies*, 179; see also 191).
33 Gérald Godin, "La folie bilinguale," *Parti pris* 3 (May 1966): 57.
34 Ibid., 56.
35 André D'Allemagne, *Le colonialisme au Québec* (Montréal: Les éditions R-B, 1966), 14.
36 Ibid., 93.
37 Ibid., 14.
38 Miron, "Le mot juste," in *L'homme rapaillé*, 237.
39 In a little-known essay, Charles Taylor draws a distinction between these two types of alienation and maintains that the *Parti pris* writers tended to ascribe to national alienation what was in fact a function of a socio-economic alienation that extended far beyond Quebec's borders. See Taylor, "La Révolution futile ou les avatars de la pensée globale," *Cité libre* 69 (August–September 1964): 10–22.
40 Andrée Fortin, *Passage de la modernité: Les intellectuels québécois et leurs revues* (Sainte-Foy: Presses de l'Université Laval, 1993), 172.

41 Bélanger, *Quatre idéologies*, 166.
42 Pierre Vallières, *White Niggers of America*, trans. Joan Pinkham (Toronto and Montreal: McClelland & Stewart, 1971), 47.
43 Ibid., 85.
44 Ibid., 149. For Vallières's phenomenological existentialist approach, see his early contributions to *Cité libre*.
45 Vallières, *White Niggers of America*, 135. He also writes: "The destiny of the Québécois collectivity had often seemed to me to be that of a people doomed to slow death, or to prolonged mediocrity. Of course I did not really dare believe that, but unconsciously this vision of the destiny of Quebec was preying on my mind" (198).
46 Pierre Vallières, *La liberté en friche* (Montréal: Québec Amérique, 1979), 9, 14.
47 In a preface written in 1979 to a later edition of *White Niggers of America*, Vallières says, "Let it suffice for me to emphasize yet again that a people as small and vulnerable as ours cannot risk its energies indefinitely without suffering serious harm in ambiguous struggles."
48 Pierre Vadeboncœur, "Critique de notre psychologie de l'action," in *Cité libre: Une anthologie*, ed. Yvan Lamonde and Gérard Pelletier (Québec: Stanké, 1991), 243.
49 Ibid., 390.
50 Serge Cantin, "Une herméneutique critique de la culture," in *L'horizon de la culture: Hommage à Fernand Dumont*, ed. Simon Langlois and Yves Martin (Sainte-Foy: Presses de l'Université Laval, 1995), 63. Dumont makes his relationship with psychoanalysis explicit in his essay collection *Le sort de la culture* (Montreal: L'Hexagone, 1987), 19, 240.
51 Fernand Dumont, *Genèse de la société québécoise* (Montréal: Boréal, 1993), 13–14.
52 "During the initial phases of the development of a collectivity, tendencies and impediments are formed which, though

they do not determine what follows according to ineluctable mechanisms, remain imperatives that underlie the constantly renewed torrent of events. As if history were situated at two levels, the sediments of the formative phase remain active under the events of subsequent periods, so that by digging down to this deep layer of history, we will have the possibility of better understanding the meaning of the present" (Dumont, *Genèse*, 331).

53 Ibid., 57.
54 Ibid., 55.
55 Ibid., 57.
56 Fernand Dumont, *Récit d'une émigration* (Montréal: Boréal, 1997), 143.
57 Dumont, *Genèse*, 133. This is the key idea of the short volume by Bouthillette, *Le Canadien français et son double*, cited above.
58 Dumont, *Genèse*, 138.
59 Ibid., 138.
60 Melancholy writers such as Jean Bouthillette and Serge Cantin take great care to specify that they do not believe the Québécois identity to be anchored in an immutable, atemporal essence. "The French-Canadian malaise is not at the level of the essential or the *in-itself*, but the relational," writes Bouthillette to Cantin, in "Lettres sur le Québec," 32.
61 Dumont, *Genèse*, 236.
62 Dumont, *Récit d'une émigration*, 129.
63 Dumont, *Genèse*, 324.
64 Ibid., 332.
65 Heinz Weinmann, "Le Québec: entre utopie et uchronie," *Liberté* 36 (April 1994): 143.
66 Dumont, *Le sort de la culture*, 242.
67 Fernand Dumont, *Raisons communes* (Montréal: Boréal, 1995), 79.
68 Ibid., 151.

69 Ibid., 27.
70 Dumont, *Genèse*, 331.
71 Ibid., 336.
72 Serge Cantin, *Ce pays comme un enfant: Essais sur le Québec (1988–1996)* (Montréal. L'Hexagone, 1997), 41.
73 Ibid., 73.
74 Serge Cantin, "Pour sortir de la survivance," *Le Devoir*, 14–15 August 1999, A9.
75 Cantin, *Ce pays comme un enfant*, 131.
76 Jocelyn Létourneau, in his essay "'Impenser' le Québec et toujours l'aimer," offers a fuller examination of the role of the nationalist intellectual belonging to a small nation. I shall return to this essay later.
77 Cantin, *Ce pays comme un enfant*, 128. He reiterates these ideas in his correspondence with Jean Bouthillette.
78 Cantin, "Pour sortir de la survivance."
79 Ibid.
80 Bouthillette and Cantin, "Lettres sur le Québec," 43; Bouthillette agrees (33).
81 Cantin, *Ce pays comme un enfant*, 131.
82 Cantin, "Pour sortir de la survivance."
83 Dumont, *Genèse*, 335.
84 Louis Cornellier, *Plaidoyer pour l'idéologie tabarnaco* (Montréal: Balzac-Le Griot, 1997), 11.
85 Louis Cornellier, "Des universitaires sur la planète Hollywood," *Le Devoir*, 12 August 1998, A6.
86 Louis Cornellier, "Contre la colonisation douce," *L'Action nationale* 88 (September 1998): 70.
87 Cornellier, *Plaidoyer*, 85.
88 However, it is difficult to be sure if this brief synopsis still corresponds to Cornellier's interpretation of the Quebec identity. In critiques of my aforementioned essay ("Authenticités québécoises") and Jocelyn Létourneau's ("Pour une révolution

de la mémoire collective"), Cornellier seems more willing to admit the non-pathological nature of multiple and ambivalent identities. See Louis Cornellier, "Identité et authenticité," *Le Devoir*, 6–7 March 1999; and "Des penseurs en revues," *Le Devoir*, 31 December 1998, D6.

89 Laurent-Michel Vacher, *Un Canabec libre: L'illusion souverainiste* (Montréal: Liber, 1991).

90 Ibid., 13 (my emphasis). In other words, independence is seen as the way to a "symbolic reconquest of national pride, a conversion from nothingness to being on the stage of historical subjectivity" (14).

91 Ibid., 15.

92 Ibid., 16–17.

93 Ibid., 23–24.

94 Translator's note: a reference to a Paul Piché song on a topic unrelated to the national question, in which the singer prefers the former option.

95 Christian Dufour, *A Canadian Challenge/Le Défi québécois* (Lantzville, BC: Oolichan Books, 1990), 18; see also 40. On the effects of the Conquest, Dufour reiterates his positions in his *La rupture tranquille* (Montréal: Boréal, 1992), 21–9. For an effective, detailed critique of Dufour's interpretation, see Dimitrios Karmis, "Interpréter l'identité québécoise," in *Québec: État et société*, ed. Alain-G. Gagnon (Montréal: Québec Amérique, 1994), 307–9.

96 Dufour, *A Canadian Challenge*, 89.

97 Karmis, "Interpréter l'identité québécoise," 309. What is more, Dufour, like Dumont and Cantin before him, uses the metaphor of the child to describe the Québécois condition. See Dufour, *A Canadian Challenge*, 63.

98 Ibid., 19.

99 Ibid., 159.

100 Jean Larose, *La petite noirceur* (Montréal: Boréal, 1987), 176.

101 Jean Larose, "Entretien," in Marcos Ancelovici and Francis Dupuis-Déri, *L'archipel identitaire: Recueil d'entretiens sur l'identité culturelle* (Montréal: Boréal, 1997), 71–2.
102 Jean Larose, *La souveraineté rampante* (Montréal: Boréal, 1994), 62.
103 Larose, *La petite noirceur*, 49; emphasis in original.
104 Ibid., 24.
105 Ibid., 165.
106 Larose, *La souveraineté rampante*, 13.
107 Ibid., 60.
108 Larose, "Entretien," 71.
109 Larose, *La petite noirceur*, 11.
110 This melancholy seems, moreover, to pervade Larose's prose a little more intensely each year. See, for example, his articles in *Le Devoir* in 1999–2000.
111 Hélène Jutras, *Quebec Is Killing Me*, trans. Hélène Jutras and Michael Gnarowski (Ottawa: Golden Dog Press, 1995), 10.
112 Ibid., 5.
113 Yvon Montoya and Pierre Thibeault, *Frénétiques* (Montréal: Triptyque, 1999), 13.
114 Ibid., 17 (my emphasis).
115 Ibid., 16 (my emphasis).
116 Ibid., 42.
117 Ibid., 89. This assertion seems quite difficult to prove historically. The identity of the Quebec francophones has taken many forms over the centuries (after all, they were "Canadiens" before there were "Canadians") and is still changing today. If Letarte is right, then there has never been a people who dragged its "ball and chain" and its "old carcass" around with such ease and agility!
118 Ibid., 106.
119 Obviously, I am not implying that the conceptions of culture brought together in *Frénétiques* constitute a monolithic bloc,

even if many of them do lack nuance and perspective. For example, Louise Dupré and Francis Dupuis-Déri, in their respective contributions, address the various tensions and the possibilities for resistance and transgression inherent in contemporary cultural identities.

120 "L'esprit d'Argument," *Argument* 1 (fall 1998): 3.
121 Daniel Tanguay, "Requiem pour un conflit générationnel," *Argument* 1 (fall 1998): 58–80.
122 "France-Québec: regards sur un éternel malentendu," *Argument* 1 (spring 1999): 18 (my emphasis).
123 Daniel Tanguay, "Un retour d'Europe," *Argument* 1 (spring 1999): 28.
124 Ibid., 32. In the same vein, playwright and director Wajdi Mouawad feels that in Quebec, "we are afraid of intelligence" (Montoya and Thibeault, *Frénétiques*, 99).
125 Tanguay, "Un retour d'Europe," 34 (my emphasis). Tanguay's paper draws heavily on an essay by André Laurendeau titled "Return from Europe," in *Witness for Quebec*, comp. and trans. Philip Stratford (Toronto: Macmillan of Canada, 1973), 213–16. Yet although Laurendeau's piece was written in 1963, he leaves much more room for doubt and nuance in his assessment of Quebec culture than does Tanguay.
126 "De la scène à la politique: Entretien avec Robert Lepage," *Argument* 1 (spring 1999): 99.
127 Jean-François Lisée, *Sortie de secours: Comment échapper au déclin du Québec* (Montréal: Boréal, 2000), 19–22; Alain Dubuc, "Penser en gagnants," *La Presse*, 22 February 2000.

CHAPTER TWO

1 For a penetrating reading of the work of Herder, see Charles Taylor, *Philosophical Arguments* (Cambridge: Harvard University Press, 1997), 79–99.

2 According to Vadeboncœur, Quebec suffers from the "malady of the servant, which is a syndrome unto itself. We are as modest as a pauper is poor. We are not sure that we have a will, because we are not sure that we are able to make use of it" (Pierre Vadeboncœur, *To be or not to be, that is the question*)*... [Montréal: Editions de l'Hexagone, 1980], 150).
3 Furthermore, it is difficult to define authenticity normatively without invoking a concept of autonomy (and vice versa). How can a human agent build an original and singular identity (authenticity) without fashioning his own laws (autonomy)? There comes a point where authenticity and autonomy interlace and practically blend into one another. On the relationship between authenticity and autonomy, see Charles Taylor, *The Malaise of Modernity* (Don Mills, Ont.: Anansi, 1991); and Alessandro Ferrara, *Reflective Authenticity: Rethinking the Project of Modernity* (London and New York: Routledge, 1998).
4 Léon Dion, "Une identité incertaine," in *L'horizon de la culture*, 467.
5 Ibid., 468.
6 Ibid., 466-9.
7 "It [the language] is the only vector of interactions and shared experiences which can nourish a *true* Quebec identity in the long term" (Gérard Bouchard, "Manifeste pour une coalition nationale," *Le Devoir*, 4-5 September 1999, A13; my emphasis).
8 Jocelyn Létourneau, "Pour une révolution de la mémoire collective: Histoire et conscience historique chez les Québécois," *Argument* 1 (fall 1998): 43.
9 Cited ibid.
10 For example, in a sentence aimed at the detractors of the modern identity, Taylor argues that "to see the full complexity and richness of the modern identity is to see, first, how

much we are all caught up in it, for all are attempts to repudiate it; and second, how shallow and partial are the one-sided judgments we make around it" (Charles Taylor, *Sources of the Self: The Making of the Modern Identity* [Cambridge: Harvard University Press, 1989], x).

11 Cantin associates the conceptualizations of the plural, hybrid nature of the Québécois identity with the passive and complacent assimilation of postmodern thought. Colonized to the marrow, Québécois intellectuals are claimed to be displaying a depressingly servile propensity to bow to an imported discourse that is now proliferating here. See Serge Cantin, "J'impense, donc j'écris: Réplique à Jocelyn Létourneau," *Argument* 1 (spring 1999): 140. Yet it has never occurred to Cantin to doubt the indigenousness of Fernand Dumont's thought, though the latter has openly acknowledged his debt to Gaston Bachelard and other foreign intellectuals.

12 Guy Laforest, *De l'urgence: Textes politiques, 1994–1995* (Montréal: Boréal, 1995), 155.

13 While Denis Monière shows how Laurendeau appropriated the heritage of Henri Bourassa and Lionel Groulx, Louis Balthazar explains the originality of Laurendeau's nationalism. See D. Monière, "André Laurendeau et le renouvellement de la pensée nationaliste," in *Penser l'éducation: Nouveaux dialogues avec André Laurendeau*, ed. Nadine Pirotte (Montréal: Boréal, 1989), 73–85; and Louis Balthazar, "André Laurendeau, un artiste du nationalisme," in *André Laurendeau: Un intellectuel d'ici*, ed. Robert Comeau and Lucille Beaudry (Québec: Presses de l'Université du Québec, 1990), 169–78.

14 As early as 1967, Laurendeau wrote, "More and more we live in pluralistic societies, wherein certain over-simplified kinds of identification become less and less possible." (Canada, *Report of the Royal Commission on Bilingualism and Biculturalism* [Ottawa: Queen's Printer, 1967–70], 1: xlviii).

15 "My stand is that Confederation is better than separation, as long as it is made over" (André Laurendeau, *Witness for Quebec*, comp. and trans. Philip Stratford [Toronto: Macmillan of Canada, 1973], 237).
16 *Report of the Royal Commission*, 1: xvii.
17 Ibid., xli.
18 Ibid., xlv.
19 Ibid., xliv. This intuition is taken up and articulated by Will Kymlicka in *Liberalism, Community and Culture* (Oxford: Clarendon Press, 1989). Alain-G. Gagnon develops this aspect of Laurendeau's thought in "La pensée politique d'André Laurendeau: Communauté, égalité et liberté," *Les cahiers d'histoire du Québec au XXe siècle* 10 (winter 2000): 31–44.
20 According to Laurendeau, francophones were right to be "furious" at this denial (Laurendeau, *Witness for Quebec*, 241).
21 Ibid., 224–8.
22 Pierre de Bellefeuille, "André Laurendeau face au séparatisme des années 60," in Comeau and Beaudry, *André Laurendeau*, 158.
23 For an overview of this research, see Guy Laforest, "Libéralisme et nationalisme au Canada," *De la prudence: Textes politiques* (Montréal: Boréal, 1993), 85–118; and François Blais, Guy Laforest, and Diane Lamoureux, eds., *Libéralismes et nationalismes: philosophie et politique* (Sainte-Foy, Presses de l'Université Laval, 1995).
24 I interpret Michel Seymour's approach as being similar; see his *La nation en question: Essai* (Montréal: L'Hexagone, 1999).
25 Laforest, *De l'urgence*, 51–63.
26 Ibid., 154.
27 Ibid., 99.
28 Pierre Vadeboncœur, *Chaque jour, indépendance* (Montréal: Leméac, 1978), 18. In the same vein: "The autonomy of the Québécois historical system has finally found a name and a

destination, and both are called independence. This has taken place under the pressure of necessity" (Vadeboncœur, *To be or not to be*, 36). Vadeboncœur reiterates this position in his recent *Gouverner ou disparaître* (Montréal: Typo, 1993).

29 Laforest, *De l'urgence*, 159.
30 Ibid., 193.
31 Ibid., 13.
32 Ibid.
33 Jean Bouthillette, *Le Canadien français et son double* (Montréal: L'Hexagone, 1972), 13.
34 Laforest, *De l'urgence*, 169.
35 Ibid., 191.
36 Ibid., 116.
37 Jocelyn Létourneau, "'Impenser' le pays et toujours l'aimer," *Cahiers internationaux de sociologie* 105 (1998): 363.
38 Cantin, "J'impense, donc j'écris," 141.
39 Létourneau, "'Impenser' le pays," 364.
40 Ibid., 380.
41 Ibid.
42 Ibid.
43 Aquin and Dumont, as fierce critiques of the Duplessis regime, must be considered Quiet Revolutionaries; but they were also critical of the Quiet Revolution's legacy. In particular, they deplored how Lesage's affirmationism and the drive to modernize Quebec tended to be founded on a denial of the past. See appendix B for more on the Quiet Revolution and affirmationism.
44 Marc Chevrier, "Our Republic in America," in *Vive Quebec! New Thinking and New Approaches to the Quebec Nation*, ed. M. Venne, trans. Robert Chodos and Louisa Blair (Toronto: James Lorimier, 2001), 92–3. In the text initially published in *Le Devoir*, Chevrier added that "while we sit by in idle discussion, the Victorian Dominion will use the opportunity to

maintain its hold, and in its eyes, Quebec will remain a crazy quilt of ethnic groups and individuals sewn onto the great fabric of a liberal, monarchist, and multicultural society" (Chevrier, "Notre république en Amérique," *Le Devoir*, 10–11 July 1999, A11).

45 James Tully, *Strange Multiplicity* (Cambridge: Cambridge University Press, 1995), 26.
46 The political philosophy writings of Charles Taylor are perhaps the exception that proves the rule in this regard.
47 See Jacques Beauchemin, "Defence and Illustration of a Nation Torn," in *Vive Quebec!*, 159.
48 Daniel Jacques, "From 'Winning Conditions' to 'Meaningful Conditions,'" in *Vive Quebec!*, 45.
49 Ibid., 44.
50 James Tully, "Introduction," in *Multinational Democracies*, ed. Alain-G. Gagnon and J. Tully (Cambridge: Cambridge University Press, 2001), 6.
51 "The challenge facing those who wish to remake the global representation of Quebec is not to arrive at a univocal vision of the nation, yesterday, today, and tomorrow. The historicity of Quebec is based on an irreducible tension among the components of Quebec society, in the same way that the identity condition of the Franco-Québécois rests on their ambivalence of being" (Jocelyn Létourneau, "Assumons l'identité québécoise dans sa complexité," *Le Devoir*, 7–8 August 1999, A9).
52 See Tully, "Introduction," *Multinational Democracies*, 2–4.
53 Létourneau, "Pour une révolution," 47.
54 Gérard Bouchard, *La nation québécoise au futur et au passé* (Montréal: VLB éditeur, 1999), 46–61.
55 Dimitrios Karmis and Jocelyn Maclure, "Two Escape Routes from the Paradigm of Monistic Authenticity: Post-Imperialist and Federal Perspectives on Plural and Complex Identities," *Ethnic and Racial Studies* 24 (May 2001): 361–85.

56 For someone like Laurent-Michel Vacher, this supple and polysemous understanding of nationalism is in fact an example of duplicity and deceit. By comparing the "pseudo" nationalism of the Québécois intellectuals to a monist, primordialist, and doctrinaire interpretation of nationalism, Vacher reaches the logical conclusion that "hardly anybody is truly – or at least overtly – nationalist in Quebec anymore." Although it is easy to understand his reasoning, given his premises, it is much harder to see why he rejects what he calls "conceptual pluralism" and objects to any attempt to reconfigure the language of nationalism in the light of contemporary phenomena such as globalization and the multiplication of collective sources of identity. Vacher proceeds as if nationalism were not a language (game) that one can modify, alter, transfigure. One may respond to his doctrinaire understanding of nationalism with a more Wittgensteinian interpretation that endeavours to grasp how the language of nationalism is transformed in its encounter with liberalism, pluralism, and globalization. See L.-M. Vacher, "Souverainisme sans nationalisme: La nouvelle trahison des clercs?" *Argument* 2 (fall 1999): 9–17. For the argument in favour of conceptual pluralism, see Michel Seymour, "Quebec and Canada at the Crossroads: A Nation within a Nation," *Nations and Nationalism* 6 (April 2000): 227–56.

57 Guy Laforest, "The Need for Dialogue and How to Achieve It," in *Beyond the Impasse: Toward Reconciliation*, ed. G. Laforest and Roger Gibbins (Montreal: Institute for Research on Public Policy, 1998), 413–28.

CHAPTER THREE

1 In a paper no doubt little known in Quebec, Maurice Charland, a professor of communication at Concordia University, offers

an interesting illustration of the textuality of identities. One can certainly challenge his idea that the Québécois identity was essentially created by the separatist rhetoric of the 1970s, epitomized in the White Paper on Sovereignty-Association of 1979. An immersion in the work of the authors discussed here shows that this identity has arisen out of a much broader and more fragmented set of phenomena. Nevertheless, by dwelling on the constitutive power of rhetorical discourses, as well as the capacity of subjects to modify and transfigure the dominant narrations of identity, Charland helps us understand the process by which identity in Quebec and collective identities in general are created. See Maurice Charland, "Constitutive Rhetoric: The Case of the *Peuple Québécois*," *Quarterly Journal of Speech* 73 (May 1987): 133–50.
2 On the relationship between nationalism and the people who endorse it, see Charles Taylor's clarifications in "Nationalism and Modernity," in *The Morality of Nationalism*, ed. Robert McKim and Jeff McMahan (New York: Oxford University Press, 1997), 31–55.
3 Ronald Rudin, *Making History in Twentieth-Century Quebec* (Toronto: University of Toronto Press, 1997), 153–98.
4 Therefore in this chapter I shall discuss the anti-nationalist, not the so-called federalist, writers. There is no need to specify that a person can very well be federalist and nationalist at the same time. In fact, this dual allegiance perhaps best epitomizes the spirit of federalism.
5 Marc Angenot and Nadia Khouri, "Quebec's Media and the Single Orthodoxy," *Cité libre* 27 (summer 1999): 6–7. In the same vein, see M. Angenot, "Les intellectuels nationalistes et la Pensée unique," *Le Devoir*, 19 July 1996, A9.
6 Obviously, it is regrettable that some replies to the arguments of people such as Hélène Jutras, René-Daniel Dubois, Esther Delisle, Mordecai Richler, Jean-Louis Roux, Guy

Bertrand, Stéphane Dion, and Marc Angenot have at times overflowed into invective and identity inflation. But it remains true that all these people have seen their ideas widely disseminated on the op-ed pages of newspapers, on radio, and on public television. The majority of them have also found publishers who, drawn to the polemical content of the works, were only too happy to publish them. One can understandably find the identity inflation practised systematically by a minority of nationalists to be exasperating, but this position too deserves to be heard. The identity inflationists are one voice among many in the polyphony of contemporary Quebec.

7 On the subject of this "dialogue of the deaf," see the incisive remarks of Alain Roy in "Identité et ressentiment," *Liberté* 40 (April 1998): 90–121.

8 See Kenneth McRoberts, "La thèse tradition-modernité: L'historique québécois," in *Les frontières de l'identité: Modernité et postmodernisme au Québec*, ed. Mikhaël Elbaz, Andrée Fortin, and Guy Laforest (Sainte-Foy: Presses de l'Université Laval, 1996), 29–45.

9 Gérard Pelletier, "*Cité libre* confesse ses intentions," in *Cité libre: Une anthologie*, ed. Yvan Lamonde and Gérard Pelletier (Montréal: Stanké, 1991), 23.

10 Gérard Pelletier and Yvan Lamonde, "Introduction," in *Cité libre: Une anthologie*, 13. Liberal individualism, then associated with an irreligious stance, could not be endorsed by the founders of *Cité libre*, who were greatly inspired by the personalism of Emmanuel Mounier.

11 André-J. Bélanger, *Quatre idéologies du Québec en éclatement: La Relève, La JEC, Cité libre, Parti pris* (Montréal: Hurtubise HMH, 1977), 81.

12 Trudeau, "Nationalist Alienation," in *Against the Current: Selected Writings, 1939–1966*, ed. Gérard Pelletier (Toronto: McClelland & Stewart, 1996), 143.

13 Pierre Elliott Trudeau, "Quebec and the Constitutional Problem," in *Federalism and the French Canadians* (Toronto: Macmillan, 1968), 5–6.
14 Trudeau, "New Treason of the Intellectuals," in *Against the Current*, 163.
15 Trudeau, "De libro, tributo ... et quibusdam aliis" and "The Practice and Theory of Federalism," in *Federalism*, 151–81.
16 Trudeau, "Nationalist Alienation," 143.
17 Ibid., 145.
18 Trudeau, "Federalism, Nationalism and Reason," in *Federalism*, 190.
19 Trudeau, "New Treason of the Intellectuals," 151.
20 Ibid., 157.
21 Trudeau, "Federalism, Nationalism and Reason," 189.
22 Ibid., 196. In the same vein, Trudeau suggests that with the progress of reason, "nationalism will have to be discarded as a rustic and clumsy tool" (202).
23 Ibid., 209.
24 For a critique of this conception of freedom, see Charles Taylor, "What's Wrong with Negative Liberty?" in *The Idea of Freedom: Essays in Honour of Isaiah Berlin*, ed. Alan Ryan (Oxford: Oxford University Press, 1979), 175–93.
25 Trudeau, "Quebec and the Constitutional Problem," 32–3.
26 "And that's why I groan when I hear calls for special status, as though we need crutches because we're not bright enough or can't protect our own language. Well, you can't have crutches against the world. You have to get out and fight" (Pierre Elliott Trudeau, *The Essential Trudeau*, ed. Ron Graham [Toronto: McClelland & Stewart 1998], 160). For a discussion of this aspect of Trudeau's political thought, see Guy Laforest, *De la prudence: Textes politiques* (Montréal: Boréal, 1993), 173–94.
27 Trudeau, "New Treason of the Intellectuals," 169.
28 Ibid., 158, 177.

29 Ibid., 181.
30 Bélanger, *Quatre idéologies*, 129.
31 Trudeau, *The Essential Trudeau*, 84 (my emphasis). Some might reply to this argument that Trudeau was himself the principal architect of a Canadian nationalism that has not lost any of its vigour today, and that is surely true. But there are nonetheless grounds for believing that in Trudeau's mind this nationalism was mainly strategic and would dissolve into a constitutional patriotism once Québécois neo-nationalism was defeated. He explains his position on the strategic legitimacy of nationalism in his essay "Federalism, Nationalism and Reason," 204.
32 The young Trudeau had nevertheless stated: "Federalism is by its very essence a compromise and a pact. It is a compromise in the sense that when national consensus on *all* things is not desirable or cannot readily obtain, the area of consensus is reduced in order that consensus on *some* things be reached. It is a pact or quasi-treaty in the sense that *the terms of that compromise cannot be changed unilaterally*" (*The Essential Trudeau*, 118; last emphasis mine). One of two conclusions is inescapable: either Trudeau had outgrown these convictions by 1982, or he believed that Quebec – a province rather than a nation – could not unilaterally block the concerted action of the federal government and the nine other provinces. On this view, the repatriation of 1982 would be unilateral only in the minds of the Québécois nationalists. I would bet on the second hypothesis.
33 *The Essential Trudeau*, 78.
34 Jean-Pierre Derriennic, *Nationalisme et démocratie: Réflexion sur les illusions des indépendantistes québécois* (Montréal, Boréal, 1995). My purpose in dwelling on Derriennic's reasoning is not to refute his anti-sovereigntist arguments point by point but, rather, to expose (in order to better criticize) his anti-nationalist ontology.

35 Ibid., 9.
36 Ibid., 22.
37 Ibid., 134.
38 Ibid., 123.
39 Ibid., 121.
40 For discussions of this genre of liberalism, see Charles Taylor, *Multiculturalism and "The Politics of Recognition,"* ed. Amy Gutmann (Princeton: Princeton University Press, 1992); and Will Kymlicka, *Contemporary Political Philosophy* (Oxford: Clarendon Press, 1990).
41 Derriennic, *Nationalisme et démocratie*, p. 38.
42 Daniel Weinstock, "La problématique multiculturaliste," in *Histoire de la philosophie politique*, vol. 5, ed. Alain Renaut with Pierre-Henri Tavoillot and Patrick Savidan (Paris: Calmann-Lévy, 1999), 452.
43 For a synopsis of the situation, see Canada, *Report of the Royal Commission on Aboriginal Peoples*, vol. 2 (Ottawa: The Commission, 1996).
44 Taiaiake Alfred, *Peace, Power, Righteousness: An Indigenous Manifesto* (Oxford: Oxford University Press, 1999).
45 For a corresponding reading, see Michael MacMillan, "La Loi sur les langues officielles et la Charte de la langue française. Vers un consensus?" Globe: *Revue internationale d'études québécoises* 2 (1999): 83–100.
46 Derriennic, *Nationalisme et démocratie*, 73–4; see also 39, 103.
47 "Nationality-based units are likely to seek different and more extensive powers than regional-based units, both because they may need greater powers to protect a vulnerable national language and culture and as a symbolic affirmation that they (unlike regional subdivisions within the majority) are 'distinct nations'" (Will Kymlicka, "Citizenship and Identity in Canada," in *Canadian Politics*, ed. James P. Bickerton and Alain-G. Gagnon [Peterborough, Ont.: Broadview Press,

1999], 24). Kymlicka believes that cultural communities can quite legitimately claim *polyethnic rights*: "These group-specific measures ... are intended to help ethnic groups and religious minorities express their cultural particularity and pride without it hampering their success in the economic and political institutions of the dominant society." The purpose of these permanent rights is to facilitate the integration of new arrivals while avoiding their outright assimilation (Will Kymlicka, *Multicultural Citizenship* [Oxford: Clarendon Press, 1995], 31).

48 In addition to the book cited in the previous note, see two others by Kymlicka: *Liberalism, Community, and Culture* (Oxford: Clarendon Press, 1991), cited previously, and *Finding Our Way: Rethinking Ethnocultural Relations in Canada* (Toronto: Oxford University Press, 1998). I cannot provide the details of my critique of the perspective developed by Kymlicka and many other contemporary political philosophers. In my view, what is now needed is for political philosophers to move from theories of justice (whether multicultural or otherwise) to (collective) practices of freedom.

49 Derriennic, *Nationalisme et démocratie*, 107, 111.

50 By way of a highly problematic demonstration, the anthropologist Claude Bariteau manages to argue for both Quebec sovereignty and the creation of an exclusively civic Quebec nation (C. Bariteau, *Québec 18 September 2001: Le monde pour horizon* [Montréal: Québec Amérique, 1998]).

51 Derriennic, *Nationalisme et démocratie*, 136 (my emphasis).

52 Marc Angenot, "Démocratie à la québécoise," *Le Devoir*, 13 June 1996, A9, and "Les intellectuels nationalistes et la Pensée unique."

53 Marc Angenot, *Les idéologies du ressentiment* (Montréal: XYZ éditeur, 1996).

54 See Jacques Pelletier, *Au delà du ressentiment: Réplique à Marc Angenot* (Montréal: XYZ éditeur, 1996); and Alain Roy,

"Identité et ressentiment," *Liberté* 40 (avril 1998): 90–121. As Roy states on page 97 of his paper, "Though starting as a work of reflection, *Les idéologies du ressentiment* metamorphoses into a diatribe; analysis gives way to polemics. This translates into a writing style pervaded with irony and agressivity."

55 Angenot, *Les idéologies du ressentiment*, 29.

56 Pelletier, *Au delà du ressentiment*, 30; Roy, "Identité et ressentiment," 94.

57 "When hopeful prospects for society are lacking, when societies find themselves faced with sustained *shortages* - whether material or ethical – individuals become disillusioned and tend to rally around identity flags steeped in rancour. That is why an analysis of the malaise in contemporary culture must not begin with resentment; it all starts with fear, the serialization of individuals, the intolerable fear of the postmodern void … The progress of resentment goes together with the withering of meaning" (Angenot, *Les idéologies du ressentiment*, 42–3).

58 For different views on the metaphysical degradation of the world, see Jean-François Lyotard, *The Postmodern Condition: A Report on Knowledge*, trans. Geoff Bennington and Brian Massumi (Manchester: Manchester University Press, 1984); Alain Touraine, *Critique of Modernity*, trans. David Macey (Cambridge, Mass.: Blackwell, 1995); and David Owen, *Maturity and Modernity: Nietzsche, Weber, Foucault and the Ambivalence of Reason* (London: Routledge, 1994).

59 Angenot, *Les idéologies du ressentiment*, 32. In the same vein, Nadia Khouri maintains that "rootedness as a value becomes a *refuge* from discontinuity and turmoil; it becomes the dogmatic incarnation of a source and a resource, and represents stability in the face of loss" ("Discours et mythes de l'ethnicité," in *Discours et mythes de l'ethnicité*, ed. Nadia Khouri [Montréal: Association canadienne-française pour l'avancement des sciences, 1992]).

60 Angenot, *Les idéologies du ressentiment*, 96 (emphasis in original).
61 Ibid., 98.
62 Ibid., 154.
63 Ibid., 61.
64 Ibid., 45 (my emphasis).
65 This is why one cannot help noticing the complicities and confluences between the agendas of Habermas and Angenot. Angenot, like Foucault, and no doubt for good reasons, criticizes the restrictiveness of the Habermasian discourse ethics, and there are certainly important nuances between their positions; but on the whole it remains a family quarrel. Angenot and Habermas share the same regulative ideal: to finish the project of modernity (ibid., 168–9; and Jürgen Habermas, *The Philosophical Discourse of Modernity: Twelve Lectures*, trans. Frederick G. Lawrence [Cambridge: MIT Press, 1987]). For critical reflections on Habermas, see Luc Langlois, "L'impératif catégorique ou le principe 'U'? De quelques objections à la Diskursethik de Habermas," in *Le prisme kantien*, ed. F. Duchesneau (Paris: Vrin, 2000); and *Foucault contra Habermas*, ed. Samantha Ashenden and D. Owen (London: Sage, 1999).
66 Angenot, *Les idéologies du ressentiment*, 166.
67 "Exaltation of 'collective rights,' which must be understood as the right to normalize in the name of collective myths and to suppress dissidence" (ibid., 107).
68 Ibid., 160.
69 Quebec political philosophers besides Taylor, including Daniel Weinstock, Dominique Leydet, Guy Laforest, Michel Seymour, Geneviève Nootens, Alan Patten, Dimitrios Karmis, and many others, are pursuing and helping to advance this line of thinking. Thus it is difficult to see why Régine Robin considers that "while English Canada has made major contributions to a

post-liberal ethics of the community, such work of philosophical exploration has hardly any equivalent in francophone Quebec" (Régine Robin, "Défaire les identités fétiches," in *La question identitaire au Canada francophone: Récits, parcours, enjeux, hors lieu*, ed. Jocelyn Létourneau [Sainte-Foy: Presses de l'Université Laval, 1994]).

70 Régine Robin, "Vieux schnock humaniste cultivé et de gauche cherche coin de terre pour continuer à penser. Nationalistes s'abstenir. Répondre au journal Spirale. Discrétion non assurée," *Spirale* 150 (September-October 1996): 4 (emphasis in original). In the same vein, see her interview with Yvon Montoya and Pierre Thibeault in *Frénétiques* (Montréal: Triptyque, 1999), 128.

71 I agree that identities are most often multiple and labile. However, this ontic position is not necessarily ontologically defensible. The fragmentation and pluralization of identities are *potentialities*. Identities, even when fashioned out of difference, may tend towards an ideal (that is increasingly difficult to attain) of unity, integrity, cohesion, suitability. In other words, individuals may present themselves as holders of an integrated, architectonic identity without thereby displaying bad faith or false consciousness. Ontologically, one cannot go much further than to state that identities are intrinsically narrative.

72 Régine Robin, "L'impossible Québec pluriel: La fascination de 'la souche,'" in *Les frontières de l'identité*, 304.

73 Robin, "Défaire les identités fétiches," 229.

74 Robin, "L'impossible Québec pluriel," 296.

75 Robin, "Défaire les identités fétiches," 216.

76 A novel of historical memory is embodied in the "various forms of collective appropriation of the past, from official history to the fictionalizing accounts offered by literature, from the learned history produced by historians to the historical

memories of minority and generational groups" (ibid., 218). For a more complete definition, see her *Le roman mémoriel: De l'histoire à l'écriture du hors-lieu* (Longueuil: Le Préambule, 1989).
77 Robin, "Défaire les identités fétiches," 220.
78 Régine Robin, *The Wanderer,* trans. Phyliss Aronoff (Montreal: Alter Ego Editions, 1997), 39.
79 Ibid., 107.
80 Robin, "Défaire les identités fétiches," 237.
81 "All that then remains is the livable, bearable community, that of those who are without community or who have broken away from one, who live in a non-space, who live in a position of interiority/exteriority, lag, non-coincidence, disparity" (ibid., 219).
82 Robin, "L'impossible Québec pluriel," 297, 309.
83 See, for example, Diane Lamoureux, "Agir sans 'nous,'" in *Les limites de l'identité sexuelle,* ed. D. Lamoureux (Montréal: Éditions du Remue-ménage, 1998).
84 Ibid., 309.
85 Robin, "Défaire les identités fétiches," 238.

CHAPTER FOUR

1 For slightly different interpretations of the concept of "community of conversation," see Jeremy Webber, *Reimagining Canada: Language, Culture, Community, and the Canadian Constitution* (Montreal and Kingston: McGill-Queen's University Press, 1994).
2 The first part of this chapter is based on the first section of the paper I wrote with Dimitri Karmis, "Two Escape Routes from the Paradigm of Monistic Authenticity: Post-Imperialist and Federal Perspectives on Plural and Complex Identities," *Ethnic and Racial Studies* 24 (May 2001): 361–85; cited previously.

3 Stuart Hall, "Who Needs Identity?" in *Questions of Cultural Identity*, ed. S. Hall and Paul du Gay (London: Sage, 1996), 2.
4 For an effective critique of Marxist reductionism, see Ernesto Laclau and Chantal Mouffe, *Hegemony and Socialist Strategy* (London: Verso, 1985); and Danielle Juteau, *L'ethnicité et ses frontières* (Montréal: Presses de l'Université de Montréal, 1999).
5 Benedict Anderson, *Imagined Communities* (London and New York: Verso, 1991), 10.
6 Craig Calhoun, "Nationalism and Civil Society," in *Social Theory and the Politics of Identity*, ed. C. Calhoun (Oxford: Blackwell, 1994), 331. See also his *Nationalism* (Buckingham: Open University Press, 1997).
7 Homi Bhabha, *The Location of Culture* (London: Routledge, 1994), 145, 158.
8 Étienne Balibar is therefore right when he asserts that "the nation as such, a political institution that is always virtually profane even when separation of church and state is not officially proclaimed, *is not sufficient* to totalize or hegemonize discourses, practices, forms of individuality ('language games' and 'forms of life' in Wittgensteinian terminology), even though it has shown itself to be incomparably more efficient than any universal religion in the reduction of 'communitarian belongings'" ("Culture and Identity (Working Notes)," in *The Identity in Question*, ed. John Rajchman [London and New York: Routledge], 181). See also Beauchemin, "Defence and Illustration of a Nation Torn," in *Vive Quebec! New Thinking and New Approaches to the Quebec Nation*, ed. Michel Venne, trans. Robert Chodos and Louisa Blair (Toronto: James Lorimer, 2001), 163.
9 Sherry Simon et al., *Fictions de l'identitaire au Québec* (Montreal: XYZ éditeur), 1991, 26.
10 James Tully, *Strange Multiplicity* (Cambridge: Cambridge University Press, 1995), 11; my parenthesis.

Notes to pages 123–5

11 James Clifford, *Routes: Travel and Translation in the Late Twentieth Century* (Cambridge, Mass.: Harvard University Press, 1997), 24.
12 This is what William Connolly calls the "self-reassurance of identity through the construction of otherness" (*Identity/Difference: Democratic Negotiations of Political Paradox* [Ithaca: Cornell University Press, 1991], 9).
13 Rob Walker, a professor of political theory at the University of Victoria, has shown how the "realist" argument in international relations to the effect that only chaos and anarchy can characterize an international order composed of nation-states is in fact based on the Hobbesian spatial resolution of the problem of authority. See R.B.J. Walker, *Inside/Outside: International Relations as Political Theory* (Cambridge: Cambridge University Press, 1993).
14 Edward W. Said, *Orientalism* (New York: Vintage Books 1979), 26.
15 Ibid., 3.
16 Ibid., 40.
17 Georg Wilhelm Hegel, *Elements of the Philosophy of Right*, ed. Allen W. Wood, trans. H.B. Nisbet (Cambridge and New York: Cambridge University Press, 1991).
18 Hall, "Who Needs Identity?" 4.
19 Jacques Derrida, *The Other Heading: Reflections on Today's Europe*, trans. Pascale-Anne Brault and Michael B. Nass (Bloomington: Indiana University Press, 1992), 9–10. Here we have an inkling of why Bouthillette, in expressing his hope that French Canadians will once again become identical to themselves, condemned himself to perpetual disappointment: "We have not disappeared, but we are no longer identical with ourselves" (Jean Bouthillette, *Le Canadien français et son double* [Montréal: L'Hexagone, 1972], 25). Note that Derrida is applying to the concept of cultural identity Wittgenstein's

insight: "'A thing is identical with itself.' There is no finer example of a useless proposition, which yet is connected with a certain play of the imagination" (L. Wittgenstein, *Philosophical Investigations*, trans. G.E.M. Anscombe [Oxford: Basil Blackwell, 1967], 84, par. 216).
20 Homi Bhabha and Jonathan Rutherford, "The Third Space: Interview with Homi Bhabha," in *Identity: Community, Culture, Difference*, ed. Jonathan Rutherford (London: Lawrence & Wishart, 1990), 208.
21 Clifford, *Routes*, 246.
22 Josée Bergeron, "Identité choisie, imposée, suggérée," *Francophonies d'Amérique* 9 (1999): 154.
23 Arjun Appadurai, *Modernity at Large: Cultural Dimensions of Globalization* (Minneapolis: University of Minnesota Press, 1996), 33.
24 Bhabha, *The Location of Culture*, 150.
25 "Each time the encounter with identity occurs at the point at which something exceeds the frame of the image, it eludes the eye, evacuates the self as site of identity and autonomy and – most important – leaves a persistent trace, a stain of the subject, a sign of resistance. We are no longer confronted with an ontological problem of being but with the discursive strategy of the moment of interrogation" (ibid., 49).
26 Charles Taylor, *Hegel and Modern Society* (Cambridge and New York: Cambridge University Press, 1979), 83.
27 Ibid., 93.
28 Ibid., 81.
29 Daniel Jacques, *Nationalité et modernité* (Montreal: Boréal, 1998), 19 (my emphasis).
30 Jacques specifies more than once that he assigns no value to the nation *in itself*. The nation as a form of political organization is "historically contingent," and consequently its defence inevitably depends on context.

31 Jacques, *Nationalité et modernité*, 226.
32 Jacques, "From 'Winning Conditions,'" in *Vive Quebec! New Thinking and New Approaches to the Quebec Nation*, ed. Michel Venne, trans. Robert Chodos and Louisa Blair (Toronto: James Lorimer, 2001), 48. See also Michel Venne, "La fin d'un faux débat entre nationalismes civique et ethnique," *Le Devoir*, 14 April 2000.
33 As Lilanne Krosenbrick-Gelissen posits, "Indian women encounter special conflicts and dilemmas in trying to reconcile, as aboriginal persons and as women, their self-government aspirations and their sexual equality aspirations" ("The Canadian Constitution, the Charter, and Aboriginal Women's Rights: Conflicts and Dilemmas," *International Journal of Canadian Studies*, spring 1993, 208).
34 "The heroism of political identity has had its day. One asks what one is, moment by moment, of the problems with which one grapples: how to take part and take sides without being taken in. Experience with, rather than engagement in" (Michel Foucault, "For an Ethic of Discomfort," in *Essential Works of Foucault, 1954–1984*, vol. 3, ed. James D. Faubion, trans. Robert Hurley for this essay [New York: New Press, 1997–2000], 445).
35 For a view that is complementary to mine in many respects, see Geneviève Nootens, "L'identité postnationale: Itinéraire(s) de la citoyenneté dans la modernité avancée," *Politique et Sociétés* 18 (1999): 99–120.
36 Nancy Huston, *Pour un patriotisme de l'ambiguïté* (Montréal: Fides, 1995).
37 Clifford, *Routes*, 36.
38 As Michel Venne suggests, "we are all *pure laine*. Some of us were knitted here. Others are *pure laine* knitted elsewhere. The wool of the first group is no purer than that of the second." Moreover, being *pure laine*, that is, an authentic subject,

does not exclude *métissage* and hybridity; quite the contrary. See Michel Venne, "Nous sommes tous des pure-laine," *Le Devoir*, 18 October 1999, A6.
39 Connolly, *Identity/Difference*, 159.
40 For example, Simon suggests "that by challenging categories constructed as entire and pure, the hybrid destabilizes certainties, creating effects of novelty and dissonance. Hybridity produces a shock, takes us by surprise, and forces us to reorient ourselves. It has the power to trouble us, and so to transform us" (Simon, *Hybridité culturelle* [Montréal: L'Ile de la tortue, 1999], 27).
41 James Tully, "Identity Politics," in *The Cambridge History of Twentieth Century Political Thought* (Cambridge: Cambridge University Press, forthcoming).
42 Translator's note: This is a reference to Denys Arcand's documentary *Le confort et l'indifférence*, which depicts the atmosphere in Quebec following the 1980 referendum.
43 See, for example, Joseph H. Carens, "Immigration, Political Community, and the Transformation of Identity: Quebec's Immigration Policies in Critical Perspective," in *Is Quebec Nationalism Just? Perspectives from Anglophone Canada* (Montreal: McGill-Queen's University Press, 1995); and Ines Molinaro, "Contexte et intégration: Les communautés allophones au Québec," *Globe* 2 (1999): 101–24.
44 Jacques Parizeau, "Lettre ouverte aux souverainistes," *Le Devoir*, 19 December 1996, A7.
45 Jacques Parizeau, *Pour un Québec souverain* (Montréal: VLB, 1997), 156 (my emphasis). Cited in Anne Trépanier, *"La grammaire générative de l'argumentaire souverainiste en 1995"* (master's thesis, Department of French Language and Literature, McGill University, 1998), 63.
46 For enlightening perspectives, see Pierre Nepveu, *L'écologie du réel: Mort et naissance de la littérature québécoise contemporaine*

(Montréal: Boréal, 1988); and Simon Harel, *Le voleur de parcours: Identité et cosmopolitisme dans la littérature québécoise contemporaine* (Montréal: Le Préambule, 1989).
47 Monique LaRue, *L'arpenteur et le navigateur* (Montréal: Fides, 1996), 8.
48 Julien Harvey, "Le Québec, société plurielle en mutation?" *Globe* 1 (1998): 43.
49 Robin, "L'impossible Québec pluriel: La fascination de 'la souche,'" in *Les frontières de l'identité: Modernité et postmodernisme au Québec*, ed. Mikhaël Elbaz, Andrée Fortin, and Guy Laforest (Sainte-Foy: Presses de l'Université Laval, 1996), 307.
50 Jocelyn Létourneau, "Rethinking Quebec (in the Canadian Landscape)," in *Vive Quebec! New Thinking and New Approaches to the Quebec Nation*, ed. Michel Venne, trans. Robert Chodos and Louisa Blair (Toronto: James Lorimer, 2001), 59.
51 Ibid., 60. Létourneau does not claim that these are hermetic worlds, but it seems to me that transcultural and hybridizing processes among these groups are more prominent than he implies. One thinks, for example, of the relations between francophones or anglophones and the many Native people living off-reserve; between non-Natives living or working in Native communities; between the large numbers of bilingual francophones and anglophones; and so on.
52 See Jocelyn Maclure, "Vers une société post-impériale," *Le Devoir*, 11 July 2000, A7; and Groupe de réflexion sur les institutions et la citoyenneté, "D'égal à égal," *Le Devoir*, 28 March 1994, A7.
53 See Daniel Salée, "La mondialisation et la construction de l'identité au Québec," in *Les frontières de l'identité*, 110–23, and "Quebec Sovereignty and the Challenge of Linguistic and Ethnocultural Minorities: Identity, Difference and the Politics of *Ressentiment*," *Quebec Studies* 24 (fall 1997): 6–23.

Notes to page 143

54 Michel Foucault, "The Ethics of the Concern for Self as a Practice of Freedom," in *Ethics: Subjectivity and Truth*, ed. Paul Rabinow, trans. P. Aranov and D. McGrawth for this essay (New York: New Press, 1997), 298.

Index

Agonized Life, The, 28, 162
allophone, 159
Anderson, Benedict, 120–1
Angenot, Marc, 11, 87, 95, 99–100, 105–12, 117
Appadurai, Arjun, 128
Aquin, Hubert, 15, 19, 22, 26–9, 37, 78, 147, 162, 163
Arendt, Hannah, 18
Argument, 58–9, 159
Assemblée Nationale. *See* National Assembly
automatism, 147, 148, 159–60, 165

Bauman, Zygmunt, 9
Bélanger, André-J., 29, 35, 89, 97
Bélanger-Campeau Commission, 6, 160–1
Benda, Julien, 94
Bergeron, Josée, 126
Bhabha, Homi, 10, 121, 129
Bill 101 (protection of the French language), 104, 153, 157
Bissoondath, Neil, 139
Borduas, Paul-Émile, 23, 148, 159, 165
Bouchard, Gérard, 20, 64, 83
Bouchard, Lucien, xii
Bourassa, Henri, 148, 161
Bourque, Gilles, 35
Bouthillette, Jean, 47, 73

British North America Act (1867), 92, 162
Brunet, Michel, 23–5, 87

Calhoun, Craig, 121
"Canadian dream" (binationalism and asymetrical federalism), 6, 75–8, 84
Cantin, Serge, 38, 46–9, 66, 76, 78, 113
Ce pays comme un enfant, 46
Chamberland, Paul, 30, 149, 163, 164
Charter of Rights and Freedoms, 5, 98–9, 132
Chen, Ying, 139
Chevrier, Marc, 45, 79–81

Index

"Chroniques du colonialisme quotidien, " 31
Cité libre, 11, 15, 26, 37, 66, 87, 89–90, 93, 99, 156, 158, 160
Clifford, James, 123, 126–7, 129, 133
Confederation (1867), 32, 96
Conquest (1760; by the British), 20, 23–4, 29, 33, 40, 47, 52, 73–4, 148
Constitution Act (1982), 6, 70
Constitution (1867), 6
Cornellier, Louis, 49
"Cultural Fatigue of French Canada, The," 26, 162

D'Allemagne, André, 32–3, 149
Derrida, Jacques, 125
Derriennic, Jean-Pierre, 15, 87, 95, 99–107, 111, 113, 117
Devoir, Le, 11, 107, 148, 153, 161
Dion, Léon, 63, 149–50
Dion, Stéphane, 99

Dubois, René-Daniel, 57, 87
Dubuc, Alain, 13, 60
Dufour, Christian, 22, 52–3
Dumont, Fernand, 10–1, 16, 22, 38–46, 77–8, 89, 99, 128, 150
Duplessis, Maurice Le Noblet, 89, 150–1, 160, 161
Durham Report, 20

Elbaz, Mikhäel, 119

Fanon, Frantz, 30–1
Federalism and the French Canadians, 92
"Federalism, Nationalism and Reason," 95
First Nations, xi, xiv, 7, 83, 98, 103–4, 133, 140–1, 143
Ford v. *P.G. Québec*, 104, 166–7
Fortin, Andrée, 34
Foucault, Michel, 12, 14, 18, 61, 83, 133
Fraser, Graham, xii
Frégault, Guy, 23–5, 33, 87, 151, 162, 163

Freud, Sigmund, 19, 48
Front de Libération du Québec (FLQ), xi, 31, 35

Genèse de la société québécoise, 22, 150
Godin, Gérald, 25, 29, 31–2, 151–2
"Great Darkness, " 89, 161–2
Groulx, Lionel, 23, 25, 34, 67, 87, 151, 152
Guevara, Che, 31

Habermas, Jürgen, 102, 109
Hall, Stuart, 120, 125
Hamelin, Jean, 91, 152
Harel, Simon, 119
Harvey, Julien, 139
Hegel, Georg Wilhelm Friedrich, 124, 129–31
Herder, Johann Gottfried von, 62
Hobbes, Thomas, 123–4

Idéologies du ressentiment, Les, 107

Jacques, Daniel, 45, 81, 131–2, 159

Index

James Bay Agreement, xiv
Juteau, Danielle, 119
Jutras, Hélène, 56

Kant, Immanuel, 61–2, 106, 129
Karmis, Dimitrios, 52, 84, 138–9
Khouri, Nadia, 87, 99, 111
Kokis, Sergio, 139
Kymlicka, Will, 105, 111

Laferrière, Dany, 139
Laforest, Guy, 6, 66–7, 69–75, 83–4, 87, 113, 119
Larose, Jean, 15, 22, 53–5, 65
LaRue, Monique, 119, 138
Laurendeau, André, 66–9, 71, 83, 87, 143, 153
Laurin, Camille, 38, 153
Lauzon, Adèle, 89, 153–4
Laval school (of historical writing), 24, 87
Léger, Jean-Marc, 89, 154
Lepage, Robert, 60

Lesage, Jean, 78, 164
Letarte, Geneviève, 58
Létourneau, Jocelyn, 10, 20, 64, 66, 75–8, 81–4, 87, 119, 140
Lévesque, René, xiv, 50–1, 67, 89, 166
Liberté, 28, 147, 155, 162
Liberté en friche, La, 37
Lisée, Jean-François, 13, 60

Maheu, Pierre, 30, 154, 163
Marcotte, Gilles, 89, 155
Marx, Karl, 30
Marxism, 34–6, 120
Meech Lake accord, 6, 20, 90
Michaud, Yves, xii–xiii
Micone, Marco, 119
Miron, Gaston, 12, 28–9, 43, 155, 162
Montoya, Yvon, 56–7
Montreal school (of historical writing), 23–5, 33, 45, 87, 148, 151, 162, 163, 167

Moutier, Maxime-Olivier, 58

National Assembly, 5, 162–3
Nationalité et modernité, 132
Native peoples. *See* First Nations
Nemni, Max, 99, 160
neo-nationalism, 157, 162, 163, 165
Nepveu, Pierre, 119, 136
New France, 20, 24, 40
"New Treason of the Intellectuals," 94
Next Episode, 27, 147, 163
Nietzsche, Friedrich, 18

Orientalism, 123
Ouellet, Fernand, 91, 155–6

Parizeau, Jacques, xii, 137
Parti pris, 11, 29–32, 34, 66–7, 87, 149, 151, 154, 155, 158, 162, 163–4
Parti Québécois (PQ), xi, 35, 161, 165, 166

Index

Péan, Stanley, 139
Pelletier, Gérard, 88–90, 99, 156, 160, 164
Pelletier, Jacques, 107–9
Plains of Abraham. *See* Conquest
Presse, La, 156, 164
Principles of the Philosophy of Right, 130

Quebec Is Killing Me, 56
"Quebec-ness" (*québecité*), 4, 15, 137, 141
Quiet Revolution, 14, 17, 32, 37, 43, 52, 57, 78, 89, 160, 161, 163, 164–5

Racine, Louis, 35
Rassemblement pour l'Indépendance Nationale (RIN), 32–3, 147, 149, 165
Rawls, John, 102
Réflexion sur les illusions des indépendantistes québécois, 100
Refus global, 23, 148, 160, 165
Renan, Ernest, 140

Rioux, Marcel, 72, 156
Robin, Régine, 16, 87, 106, 111–18, 139
Roy, Alain, 107–9
Royal Commission on Bilingualism and Biculturalism, 67, 150, 153, 156; report, 68
Rudin, Ronald, 87

Said, Edward, 123
Salée, Daniel, 119
Sauvé, Paul, 157
Séguin, Maurice, 23–5, 87, 157, 162, 163
Seymour, Michel, 11
Simon, Sherry, 119, 122–3, 128
sovereignty-association, 161, 165–6
Supreme Court of Canada, 7, 166
survivance, 162, 163, 167

Tanguay, Daniel, 59
Taylor, Charles, 6–7, 9, 18, 65, 89–90, 100, 111, 129–31, 159
Thibeault, Pierre, 56–7

Todorov, Tzvetan, 128
Trudeau, Pierre Elliott, 5, 26, 72, 89–100, 104–7, 160
Trudel, Marcel, 91, 157–8
Tully, James, 15, 18, 79–81, 111, 122–3, 128, 134

Vacher, Laurent-Michel, 50–1
Vadeboncœur, Pierre, 37, 71–2, 76, 89, 158
Vallières, Pierre, 22, 34–7, 49, 60, 89, 158, 163, 167
Venne, Michel, 132

Wanderer, The, 115
Weinmann, Heinz, 43
Weinstock, Daniel, 102–3, 105
White Niggers of America, 35–6, 158, 164, 167
White Paper (1969), 98
Wittgenstein, Ludwig, 18, 57

Young, Iris Marion, 127